Consciousness and the Unconscious

A list of Jung's works appears at the back of the volume.

Consciousness and the Unconscious

LECTURES DELIVERED AT ETH ZURICH
VOLUME 2: 1934

C. G. JUNG
EDITED BY ERNST FALZEDER

Translated by Mark Kyburz, John Peck, and Ernst Falzeder

ⓟ PHILEMON SERIES
  Published with the support of the Philemon Foundatiom
  This book is part of the Philemon Series of the Philemon Foundation

PRINCETON UNIVERSITY PRESS
PRINCETON AND OXFORD

Introduction, English translation, and scholarly apparatus copyright © 2022 by Philemon Foundation

Princeton University Press is committed to the protection of copyright and the intellectual property our authors entrust to us. Copyright promotes the progress and integrity of knowledge created by humans. By engaging with an authorized copy of this work, you are supporting creators and the global exchange of ideas. As this work is protected by copyright, any reproduction or distribution of it in any form for any purpose requires permission; permission requests should be sent to permissions@press.princeton.edu. Ingestion of any PUP IP for any AI purposes is strictly prohibited.

Published by Princeton University Press
41 William Street, Princeton, New Jersey 08540
99 Banbury Road, Oxford OX2 6JX

All illustrations are reproduced by permission of either the Jung estate or the Philemon Foundation.

press.princeton.edu

GPSR Authorized Representative: Easy Access System Europe - Mustamäe tee 50, 10621 Tallinn, Estonia, gpsr.requests@easproject.com

All Rights Reserved

First paperback printing, 2025
Paperback ISBN 9780691256061
Cloth ISBN 9780691228570
ISBN (e-book) 9780691228587
Library of Congress Control Number: 2021948192

British Library Cataloging-in-Publication Data is available

Editorial: Fred Appel and James Collier
Production Editorial: Karen Carter
Text Design: Carmina Alvarez
Jacket/Cover Design: Black Kat Design LLC
Production: Danielle Amatucci
Publicity: Kathryn Stevens

Jacket/Cover art: Robyn Parker, *Tropical Fish Wheel*. Private Collection © Robyn Parker / Bridgeman Images

This book has been composed in Sabon LT Std

Contents

General Introduction ERNST FALZEDER, MARTIN LIEBSCHER, AND SONU SHAMDASANI	vii
Editorial Guidelines	xvii
Editorial Note to this Volume	xxi
Acknowledgments	xxiii
Chronology	xxv
Introduction to Volume 2 ERNST FALZEDER	xlvii

THE LECTURES

Lecture 1 20 April 1934	1
Lecture 2 27 April 1934	10
Lecture 3 4 May 1934	17
Lecture 4 18 May 1934	25
Lecture 5 25 May 1934	34
Lecture 6 1 June 1934	41

Lecture 7 8 June 1934	49
Lecture 8 15 June 1934	57
Lecture 9 22 June 1934	65
Lecture 10 29 June 1934	74
Lecture 11 6 July 1934	83
Lecture 12 13 July 1934	91
Bibliography	103
Index	109

General Introduction

ERNST FALZEDER, MARTIN LIEBSCHER, AND SONU SHAMDASANI

BETWEEN 1933 AND 1941, C. G. Jung lectured at the Swiss Federal Institute for Technology (ETH). He was appointed a professor there in 1935. This represented a resumption of his university career after a long hiatus, as he had resigned his post as a lecturer in the medical faculty at the University of Zurich in 1914. In the intervening period, Jung's teaching activity had principally consisted in a series of seminars at the Psychology Club in Zurich, which were restricted to a membership consisting of his own students or followers. The lectures at ETH were open, and the audience for the lectures was made up of students at ETH, the general public, and Jung's followers. The attendance at each lecture was in the hundreds: Josef Lang, in a letter to Hermann Hesse, spoke of six hundred participants at the end of 1933,[1] Jung counted four hundred in October 1935.[2] Kurt Binswanger, who attended the lectures, recalled that people often could not find a seat and that the listeners "were of all ages and of all social classes: students . . . ; middle-aged people; also many older people; many ladies who were once in analysis with Jung."[3] Jung himself attributed this success to the novelty of his lectures and expected a gradual decline in numbers: "Because of the huge crowd my lectures have to be held in the *auditorium maximum*. It is of course their sensational nature that enchants people to come. As soon as people will realize that these lectures are concerned with serious matters, the numbers will become more modest."[4]

---

[1] Josef Bernhard Lang to Hermann Hesse, end of November 1933 (Hesse, 2006, p. 299).
[2] Jung (1977), p. 87.
[3] Interview with Gene Nameche [Countway Library of Medicine, Boston], p. 6.
[4] Jung to Jolande Jacobi, 9 January 1934 [Jung Archives, ETH Zurich].

Because of this context, the language of the lectures is far more accessible than Jung's published works at this time. Binswanger also noted that "Jung prepared each of those lectures extremely carefully. After the lectures, a part of the audience always remained to ask questions, in a totally natural and relaxed situation. It was also pleasant that Jung never appeared at the last minute, as so many other lecturers did. He, on the contrary, was already present before the lecture, sat on one of the benches in the corridor; and people could go and sit with him. He was communicative and open."[5]

The lectures usually took place on Fridays between 6 and 7 p.m. The audience consisted of regular students of technical disciplines, who were expected to attend additional courses from a subject of the humanities. But as it was possible to register as a guest auditor, many of those who had come to Zurich to study with Jung or undertake therapy attended the lectures as an introduction to Analytical Psychology. In addition, Jung also held ETH seminars with limited numbers of participants, in which he would further elaborate on the topics of the lectures. During the eight years of his lectures—which were only interrupted in 1937, when Jung travelled to India—he covered a wide range of topics. These lectures are at the center of Jung's intellectual activity in the 1930s, and furthermore provide the basis of his work in the 1940s and 1950s. Thus, they form a critical part of Jung's oeuvre, one that has yet to be accorded the attention and study that it deserves. The subjects that Jung addressed in ETH lectures are probably even more significant to present-day scholars, psychologists, psychotherapists, and the general public than they were when they were first delivered. The passing years have seen a mushrooming of interest in Eastern thought, Western hermeticism and mystical traditions, the rise of the psychological types industry and the dream work movement, and the emergence of a discipline of the history of psychology.

CONTENTS OF THE LECTURES

Volume 1: **History of Modern Psychology** *(Winter Semester 1933/1934)*

The first semester, from 20 October 1933 to 23 February 1934, consists of sixteen lectures on what Jung called the history of "modern psychology," by which he meant psychology as "a conscious science," not one that projects the psyche into the stars or alchemical processes, for instance. His

---

[5] Interview with Gene Nameche [Countway Library of Medicine, Boston], p. 6.

account starts at the dawn of the age of Enlightenment, and presents a comparative study of movements in French, German, and British thought. He placed particular emphasis on the development of concepts of the unconscious in nineteenth-century German Idealism. Turning to England and France, Jung traced the emergence of the empirical tradition and of psychophysical research, and how these in turn were taken up in Germany and led to the emergence of experimental psychology. He reconstructed the rise of scientific psychology in France and in the United States. He then turned to the significance of spiritualism and psychical research in the rise of psychology, paying particular attention to the work of Justinus Kerner and Théodore Flournoy. Jung devoted five lectures to a detailed study of Kerner's work, *The Seeress of Prevorst* (1829),[6] and two lectures to a detailed study of Flournoy's *From India to the Planet Mars* (1899).[7] These works initially had a considerable impact on Jung. As well as elucidating their historical significance, his consideration of them enables us to understand the role that his reading of them played in his early work. Unusually, in this section Jung eschewed a conventional history of ideas approach, and placed special emphasis on the role of patients and subjects in the constitution of psychology. In the course of his reading of these works, Jung developed a detailed taxonomy of the scope of human consciousness, which he presented in a series of diagrams. He then presented a further series of illustrative case studies of historical individuals in terms of this model: Niklaus von der Flüe, Goethe, Nietzsche, Freud, John D. Rockefeller, and the "so-called normal man."

Of the major figures in twentieth-century psychology, Jung was arguably the most historically and philosophically minded. These lectures thus have a twofold significance. On the one hand, they present a seminal contribution to the history of psychology, and hence to the current historiography of psychology. On the other hand, it is clear that the developments that Jung reconstructed teleologically culminate in his own "complex psychology" (his preferred designation for his work), and thus present his own understanding of its emergence. This account provides a critical correction to the prevailing Freudocentric accounts of the development of Jung's work, which were already in circulation at this time. The detailed taxonomy of consciousness that he presented in the second part of this semester was not documented in any of his published works. In presenting it, Jung noted that the difficulties that he had encountered with his project

---

[6] Kerner (1829).
[7] Flournoy (1900 [1899]).

for a psychological typology had led him to undertake this. Thus these lectures present critical aspects of Jung's mature thought that are unavailable elsewhere.

Volume 2: **Consciousness and the Unconscious** *(Summer Semester 1934)*

This volume presents twelve lectures from 20 April 1934 to 13 July 1934. Jung commenced with lectures on the problematic status of psychology, and attempted to give an account as to how the various views of psychology in its history, which he had presented in the first semester, had been generated. This led him to account for national differences in ideas and outlook, and to reflect on different characteristics and difficulties of the English, French, and German languages when it came to expressing psychological materials. Reflecting on the significance of linguistic ambiguity led Jung to give an account of the status of the concept of the unconscious, which he illustrated with several cases. Following these general reflections, he presented his conception of the psychological functions and types, illustrated by practical examples of their interaction. He then gave an account of his concept of the collective unconscious. Filling a lacuna in his earlier accounts, he gave a detailed map of the differentiation and stratification of its contents, in particular as regards cultural and "racial" differences. Jung then turned to describing methods for rendering accessible the contents of the unconscious: the association experiment, the psycho-galvanic method, and dream analysis. In his account of these methods, Jung revised his previous work in the light of his present understanding. In particular, he gave a detailed account of how the study of associations in families enabled the psychic structure of families and the functioning of the complexes to be studied. The semester concluded with an overview of the topic of dreams and the study of several dreams.

On the basis of his reconstruction of the history of psychology, Jung then devoted the rest of this and the following semesters to an account of his "complex psychology." As in the other semesters, Jung was confronted with a general audience, a context that gave him a unique opportunity to present a full and generally accessible account of his work, as he could not presuppose prior knowledge of psychology. Thus we find here the most detailed, and perhaps most accessible, introduction to his own theory. This is by no means just an introduction to previous work, however, but a full-scale reworking of his early work in terms of his current understanding, and it presents models of the personality that cannot be found anywhere else in his work. Thus, this volume is Jung's most up-to-date account of his theory of complexes, association experiments, understanding of dreams, the structure of the personality, and the nature of psychology.

Volume 3: **Modern Psychology and Dreams** *(Winter Semester 1934/1935 and Summer Semester 1935)*

The third volume presents lectures from two consecutive semesters: seventeen lectures from 26 October 1934 to 8 March 1935, and eleven lectures from 3 May 1935 to 12 July 1935, here collected in one volume as they all deal primarily with possible methods to access, and try to determine the content of, the unconscious. Jung starts with a detailed description of Freud's and, to a somewhat lesser extent, Adler's theory and method of analyzing dreams, and then proceeds to his own views (dreams are "pure nature" and of a complementary/compensatory character) and technique (context, amplification). He focuses particularly on three short dream series, the first from the Nobel Prize winner Wolfgang Pauli, the second from a young homosexual man, and the third from a psychotic person, using them to describe and interpret special symbolisms. In the following semester, he concludes the discussion of the mechanism, function, and use of dreams as a method to enlighten us and to get to know the unconscious, and then draws attention to "Eastern parallels," such as yoga, while warning against their indiscriminate use by Westerners. Instead he devotes the rest of the semester to a detailed example of "active imagination," or "active phantasizing," as he calls it here, with the help of the case of a fifty-five-year-old American lady, the same case that he discussed at length in the German seminar of 1931.

This volume gives a detailed account of Jung's understanding of Freud's and Adler's dream theories, shedding interesting light on the points in which he concurred and in which he differed, and how he developed his own theory and method in contradistinction to those. Since he was dealing with a general audience, a fact that he was very much aware of, he tried to stay on a level as basic as possible—which is also of great help to the contemporaneous, nonspecialized reader. This is also true for his method of active imagination, as exemplified in one long example. Although he used material also presented elsewhere, the present account is highly interesting precisely because it is tailored to a most varied general audience, and differs accordingly from presentations given to the handpicked participants in his "private" seminars, or in specialized books.

Volume 4: **Psychological Typology** *(Winter Semester 1935/1936 and Summer Semester 1936)*

The fourth volume also combines lectures from two semesters: fifteen lectures from 25 October 1935 to 6 March 1936, and thirteen lectures from 1 May 1936 to 10 July 1936. The winter semester gives a general introduction to the history of typologies, and typology in intellectual and religious history, from antiquity to Gnosticism and Christianity, from Chinese philosophy (yin/yang) to Persian religion and philosophy (Ahriman/Lucifer), from the French revolution ("déesse raison") to Schiller's *Letters on the Aesthetic Education of Man*. Jung introduces and describes in detail the two attitudes (introversion and extraversion) and the four functions (thinking and feeling as rational functions, sensation and intuition as irrational functions). In the summer semester, he focuses on the interplay between the attitudes and the various functions, detailing the possible combinations (extraverted and introverted feeling, thinking, sensation, and intuition) with the help of many examples.

This volume offers an excellent, first-hand introduction to Jung's typology, and is *the* alternative for contemporaneous readers who are looking for a basic, while authentic text, as opposed to Jung's magnum opus *Psychological Types*, which, as it were, hides the sleeping beauty behind a thick wall of thorny bushes, namely, its 400 plus pages of "introduction," only after which Jung deals with his own typology proper. As in the previous volumes, readers will benefit from the fact that Jung was compelled to give a basic introduction to and overview of his views.

Volume 5: **Psychology of the Unconscious** *(Summer Semester 1937 and Summer Semester 1938)*

Jung dedicated his lectures of summer 1937 (23 April–9 July; eleven lectures) and summer 1938 (29 April–8 July; ten lectures) to the psychology of the unconscious. The understanding of the sociological and historical dependency of the psyche and the relativity of consciousness form the basis to familiarize the audience with different manifestations of the unconscious related to hypnotic states and cryptomnesia, unconscious affects and motivation, memory and forgetting. Jung shows the normal and pathological forms of invasions of unconscious contents into consciousness and outlines the methodologies to bring unconscious material to the surface. This includes methods such as the association experiment, dream analysis, active imagination, as well as different forms of creative expression, but also ancient tools of divination, including astrology and the I-Ching. The summer semester of 1938 returned to the dream series of the young homosexual man discussed in detail in the lectures of 1935, this time highlighting Jung's method of dream interpretation on an individual and a symbolic level.

Jung illustrates his lectures with several diagrams and clinical cases to make it more accessible to nonpsychologists. In some instances the lectures provide welcome additional information to published articles, as Jung was not obliged to restrict his material to a confined space. For example, Jung elaborated on the famous case of the so-called moon-patient, which was so important for his understanding of psychic reality and psychosis, or gave a very personal introduction to the usage of the I-Ching. The lectures also shed a new historical light on his journeys to Africa, India, and New Mexico and his reception of psychology, philosophy, and literature.

Volume 6: **Psychology of Yoga and Meditation** *(Winter Semester 1938/1939 and Summer Semester 1939; plus the First Two Lectures of the Winter Semester 1940/1941)*

The lecture series of the winter semester 1938/1939 (28 October–3 March; fifteen lectures) and the first half of the summer semester 1939 (28 April–9 June; six lectures) are concerned with Eastern spirituality. Starting out with the psychological concept of active imagination, Jung seeks to find parallels in Eastern meditative practices. His focus is directed on meditation as taught by different yogic traditions and in Buddhist practice. The texts for Jung's interpretation are Patanjali's *Yoga Sûtra*, according to the latest research written around 400 CE[8] and regarded as one of the most important sources for our knowledge of yoga today, the *Amitâyur-Dhyâna-Sûtra* from the Chinese Pure Land Buddhist tradition, translated from Sanskrit to Chinese by Kâlayasas in 424 CE,[9] and the *Shrî-chakra-sambhâra Tantra*, a scripture related to tantric yoga, translated and published in English by Arthur Avalon (Sir John Woodroffe) in 1919.[10]

Nowhere else in Jung's works can one find such detailed psychological interpretations of those three spiritual texts. In their importance for understanding Jung's take on Eastern mysticism, the lectures of 1938/39

---

[8] Maas (2006).
[9] Müller (1894), pp. xx–xxi.
[10] Avalon (1919).

can only be compared to his reading of the *Secret of the Golden Flower*[11] or the seminars on Kundalini Yoga.[12]

In the winter semester 1940/41, Jung summarizes the arguments of his lectures on Eastern meditation. The summary is published as an addendum at the end of this volume.

Volume 7: Spiritual Exercises of Ignatius of Loyola *(Summer Semester 1939 and Winter Semester 1939/1940; in Addition: Lecture 3, Winter Semester 1940/1941)*

The second half of the summer semester 1939 (16 June–7 July; four lectures) and the winter semester 1939/40 (3 October–8 March; sixteen lectures) were dedicated to the *Exercitia Spiritualia*[13] of Ignatius of Loyola, the founder and first general superior of the Society of Jesus (Jesuits). As a knight and soldier, Ignatius was injured in the battle of Pamplona (1521), in the aftermath of which he experienced a spiritual conversion. Subsequently he renounced his worldly life and devoted himself to the service of God. In March 1522, the Virgin Mary and the infant Jesus appeared to him at the shrine of Montserrat, which led him to search for solitude in a cave near Manresa. There he prayed for seven hours a day and wrote down his experiences for others to follow. This collection of prayers, meditations, and mental exercises built the foundation of the *Exercitia Spiritualia* (1522–1524). In the text, Jung saw the equivalent to the meditative practice of the Eastern spiritual tradition. He provides a psychological reading of it, comparing it to the modern Jesuit understanding of theologians like Erich Przywara.

Jung's considerations on the *Exercitia Spiritualia* follow the lectures on Eastern meditation of the previous year. Nowhere in Jung's writings is there to be found a similarly intense comparison between oriental and occidental spiritualism. Its approach equals the aim of the annual Eranos conference, namely to open up a dialogue between the East and the West. Jung's critical remarks about the embrace of Eastern mysticism by modern Europeans and his suggestion to the latter to come back to their own traditions are illuminated through those lectures.

In the winter semester 1940/1941, Jung dedicated the third lecture to a summary of his lectures on the *Exercitia Spiritualia*. This summary is added as an addendum to volume 7.

---

[11] Jung (1929).
[12] Jung (1932).
[13] Ignatius of Loyola (1996 [1522–1524]).

Volume 8: **The Psychology of Alchemy** *(Winter Semester 1940/1941 and Summer Semester 1941)*

The lectures of the winter semester 1940/41 (from lecture 4 onward; 29 November–28 February; twelve lectures) and the summer semester 1941 (2 May–11 July; eleven lectures) provide an introduction to Jung's psychological understanding of alchemy. He explained the theory of alchemy, outlined the basic concepts, and gave an account of psychological research into alchemy. He showed the relevance of alchemy for the understanding of the psychological process of individuation. The alchemical texts that Jung talked about included, next to famous examples such as the *Tabula Smaragdina* and the *Rosarium Philosophorum*, many less well-known alchemical treatises.

The lectures on alchemy built a cornerstone in the development of Jung's psychological theory. His Eranos lectures from 1935 and 1936 were dedicated to the psychological meaning of alchemy and were later merged together in *Psychology and Alchemy* (1944). The ETH lectures on alchemy highlight the way Jung's thinking of alchemy developed through those years. As an introduction to alchemy, they provide an indispensable tool in order to understand the complexity of his late works such as *Mysterium Coniunctionis*.

REFERENCES

Avalon, Arthur [Sir John Woodroffe] (ed.) (1919). *Shrî-chakra-sambhâra Tantra*. Trans. Kazi Dawa-Samdup. *Tantrik Texts*, vol. 7. London: Luzac & Co; Calcutta: Thacker, Spink & Co.

Flournoy, Théodore (1900 [1899]). *Des Indes à la planète Mars. Étude sur un cas de somnambulisme avec glossolalie*. Paris, Geneva: F. Alcan, Ch. Eggimann. *From India to the Planet Mars. A Case of Multiple Personality with Imaginary Languages*. With a Foreword by C. G. Jung and Commentary by Mireille Cifali. Ed. and introduced by Sonu Shamdasani. Princeton: Princeton University Press, 1994.

Hesse, Hermann (2006 [1916–1944]). *"Die dunkle und wilde Seite der Seele": Briefwechsel mit seinem Psychoanalytiker Josef Bernhard Lang 1916–1944*. Ed. Thomas Feitknecht. Frankfurt am Main: Suhrkamp.

(Saint) Ignatius of Loyola (1996 [1522–1524]). *The Spiritual Exercises*, in *Personal Writings: Reminiscences, Spiritual Diary, Selected Letters Including the Text of The Spiritual Exercises*. Trans. with introductions and notes by Joseph A. Munitiz and Philip Endean. London: Penguin, pp. 281–328.

Jung, C. G. (1929). Commentary on "The Secret of the Golden Flower." CW 13.

Jung, C. G. (1932). *The Psychology of Kundalini Yoga: Notes of the Seminar Given in 1932 by C. G. Jung*. Ed. Sonu Shamdasani. Bollingen Series XCIX. Princeton: Princeton University Press, 1996.

Kerner, Justinus Andreas Christian (1829). *Die Seherin von Prevorst. Eröffnungen über das innere Leben und über das Hineinragen einer Geisterwelt in die unsere*. Two vols. Stuttgart, Tubingen: J. G. Cotta'sche Buchhandlung. 4., vermehrte und verbesserte Auflage: Stuttgart, Tubingen: J. G. Cotta'scher Verlag. Reprint: Kiel: J. F. Steinkopf Verlag, 2012. *The Seeress of Prevorst, Being Revelations Concerning the Inner-Life of Man, and the Inter-Diffusion of a World of Spirits in the One We Inhabit*. Trans. Catherine Crowe. London: J. C. Moore, 1845. Digital reprint: Cambridge: Cambridge University Press, 2011.

Maas, Philipp A. (2006). *Samâdhipâda: das erste Kapitel des Pâtañjalayogaśâstra zum ersten Mal kritisch ediert*. Aachen: Shaker.

Müller, Max (1894). *Introduction to Buddhist Mahâyâna Texts, The Sacred Books of The East*, vol. 49. Ed. Max Müller. Oxford: The Clarendon Press.

Editorial Guidelines

WITH THE EXCEPTION of a few preparatory notes, there is no written text by Jung. The present text has been reconstructed by the editors through several notes by participants of Jung's lectures. Through the use of shorthand, the notes taken by Eduard Sidler, a Swiss engineer, and Rivkah Schärf—who later became a well-known religious scholar, psychotherapist, and collaborator of Jung—provide a fairly accurate first basis for the compilation of the lectures. (The shorthand method used is outdated and had to be transcribed by experts in the field.)

Together with the recently discovered scripts by Otto Karthaus, who made a career as one of the first scientific vocational counselors in Switzerland, Bertha Bleuler, and Lucie Stutz-Meyer, the gymnastic teacher of the Jung family, these notes enable us to not only regain access to the contents of Jung's orally delivered lectures, but also to get a feeling for the fascination of the audience with Jung the orator.

There also exists a set of mimeographed notes in English that have been privately published and circulated in limited numbers. They were edited and translated by an English-speaking group in Zurich around Barbara Hannah and Elizabeth Welsh, and present more of a résumé than an attempt at a verbatim account of the content of the lectures. For the first years Hannah's edition relied only on the notes by Marie-Jeanne Schmid, Jung's secretary at the time; for the later lectures the script of Rivkah Schärf provided the only source for most of the text. The edition was disseminated in private imprints from 1938 to 1968.

The Hannah edition does deviate from Jung's original spoken text as recorded in the other notes. Hannah and Welsh stated in their "Prefatory Note" that their compilation did "not claim to be a verbatim report or literal translation." Hannah was mainly interested in the creation of a readable and consistent text and did not shy away from adding or omitting passages for that purpose. As her edition was only based on one set of notes, she could not correct passages where Schmid or Schärf rendered

Jung's text wrongly. But as Hannah had the advantage of talking to Jung in person, when she was not sure about the content of a certain passage, her English compilation is sometimes useful to provide additional information to the readers of our edition.

In contrast to a critical edition, it is not intended to provide the differing variations in a separate critical apparatus. Had we faithfully listed all the minor or major variants in the scripts, the text would have become virtually unreadable and thus would have lost the accessibility that is the hallmark of Jung's presentation. For the most part, however, we can be reasonably certain that the compilation accurately reflects what Jung said, although he may have used different words or formulations. Moreover, in quite a number of key passages it was even possible to reconstruct the verbatim content, for example, when different note takers identified certain passages as direct quotes. Variations often do not add to the content and intelligibility, and often originated in errors or lack of understanding by the participant taking notes. In their compilation, the editors have worked according to the principle that as much information as possible should be extracted from the manuscripts. If there are obvious contradictions that cannot be decided by the editor, or, as might be the case, clear errors on behalf of Jung or the listener, it will be clarified by the editor's annotation.

Of the note takers, Eduard Sidler, whose background was in engineering, had the least understanding of Jungian psychology at the beginning, although naturally he became more familiar with Jungian psychology over time. In any case, he did try to protocol faithfully as much as he could, making his the most detailed notes. Sometimes he could no longer follow, however, or clearly misunderstood what was said. On the other hand, we have Welsh and Hannah's version, which in itself was already a collation and obviously heavily edited but is (at least for the first semesters) the most consistent manuscript and also contains things that are missing in other notes. Moreover, they state that "Prof. Jung himself ... has been kind enough to help us with certain passages," although we do not know which these are. In addition, over the course of the years, and also for individual lectures, the quality, accuracy, and reliability of the scripts by the different note takers vary, as is only natural. In short, the best we can do is try and find an approximation of what Jung actually said. In essence, it will always have to be a judgment call how to collate those notes.

It is thus impossible to establish exact editorial principles for each and every situation, so that different editors would inevitably arrive at exactly the same formulations. We could only adhere to some general guidelines, such as "Interfere as little as possible, and as much as necessary," or "Try to establish what the most likely thing was that Jung might have said, on the basis of all the sources available" (including the *Collected Works*, autobiographical works or interviews, other seminars, interviews, etc.). If two transcripts concur, and the third is different, it is usually safe to go with the first two. In some cases, however, it is clear from the context that the two are wrong, and the third is correct. Or if all three of them are unclear, it is sometimes possible to "clean up" the text by having recourse to the literature; for instance, when Jung summarizes Kerner's story of the Seeress of Prevorst. As with all scholarly works of this kind, there is no explicit recipe that can be fully spelled out: One has to rely on one's scholarly judgement.

These difficulties not only concern the establishment of the text of Jung's ETH lectures, but also pertain to notes of his seminars in general, many of which have already appeared in print without addressing this problem. For instance, the introduction to the *Dream Analysis* seminar mentions the number of people that were involved in preparing the notes, but there is no account of how they worked, or how they established the text (Jung, 1984, pp. x–xi). Some manuscript notes in the library of the Analytical Psychology Club in Los Angeles indicate that the compilation of the notes involved significant "processing by committee." It is interesting in this regard to compare the sentence structure of the *Dream Analysis* seminar with the 1925 seminar, which was checked by Jung. On 19 October 1925, Jung wrote to Cary Baynes, after checking her notes and acknowledging her literary input: "I faithfully worked through the notes as you will see. I think they are as a whole very accurate. Certain lectures are even fluent, namely those which you could not stop your libido from flowing in" (Cary Baynes papers, contemporary medical archives, Wellcome Library, London).

Our specific situation seems to be a "luxury" problem, as it were, because we have several transcripts, which was often not the case in other seminars. We also have the disadvantage of no longer being able to ask Jung himself, as for instance Cary Baynes, Barbara Hannah, Marie-Jeanne Schmid, or Mary Foote could do. We can only work as best we can, and caution the reader that there is no guarantee that this is "verbatim Jung," although we have tried to come as close as possible to what he actually said.

Editorial Note to this Volume

THE TEXT OF the following lectures is a reconstruction, based on original shorthand notes by Eduard Sidler and Rivkah Kluger-Schärf, both in the original German, as well as on Barbara Hannah's compilation in English (Hannah, 1959 [=Hannah]),[14] about which she wrote in her preface: "Elizabeth Welsh, Una Thomas and I recorded [the lectures] to the best of our ability in English. . . . We had our own notes to work on, and the benefit of Frau Dr. Marie-Jeanne Boller-Schmid's and Frau Dr. Riwkah Kluger-Schärf's German stenograms" (p. 7; Schmid's original notes for this volume are no longer extant and could not be used for the purpose of comparison). Hannah also notes that "none of [her] editions has been revised by Prof. Jung himself" (p. 7), although "he has been kind enough to help us with certain passages" (p. 6).

While Hannah's text aims "at giving a clear outline of the main content of each lecture," it does "not claim to be a verbatim report or literal translation" (p. 6). The process of condensation—and also of translation—sometimes loses nuances, finer points, or digressions by Jung. In general, the German notes, especially those by Sidler, are more detailed and try to follow the spoken word as closely as possible. In some instances, Sidler and Schärf even put phrases in quotation marks to indicate that these were indeed Jung's words. On the other hand, however, they are also sometimes incomplete or fragmentary—for instance, when they could not keep pace or clearly misunderstood/misheard Jung—or even missing. In these cases, I had to have recourse to Hannah's version, and, whenever this concerned a more significant point, or a somewhat longer passage, this is indicated in a footnote.

Thanks to Sonu Shamdasani, Martin Liebscher, and Chris Wagner for the ongoing collegial exchange and help. Thanks to Thomas Fischer for his

---

[14] The notes were privately printed, and "strictly intended for private use" (p. 7). They will be quoted henceforth as simply "Hannah, [page number]."

support throughout and for his help with specific points. Special thanks are due to Ulrich Hoerni, who, with his intimate knowledge of the lecture notes since their rediscovery and the specific Swiss variant of "High" German in which Jung spoke, went over the German manuscript with a very fine-toothed comb and made many valuable suggestions.

Ernst Falzeder

Acknowledgments

THE PREPARATION FOR PUBLICATION OF THESE LECTURES, from thousands of pages of auditors' notes, has had a long gestation. Like a complex jigsaw puzzle assembled by numerous hands over many years, this work would not have been possible without the contributions of many individuals, to whom thanks are due. The Philemon Foundation, under its past presidents Steve Martin, Judith Harris, and Richard Skues, past copresident, Nancy Furlotti, and present president, Caterina Vezzoli, has been responsible for this project since 2004. Without the contributions of its donors, none of the editorial work would have been possible or come to fruition. From 2012 to 2020, the project was supported by Judith Harris at UCL. From 2004 to 2011, the project was principally supported by Carolyn Fay, the C. G. Jung Educational Center of Houston, the MSST Foundation, and the Furlotti Family Foundation. The project was also supported by research grants from the International Association for Analytical Psychology in 2006, 2007, 2008, and 2009.

This publication project was commenced by the former Society of Heirs of C. G. Jung (now the Foundation of the Works of C. G. Jung), between 1993 and 1998. Since its inception, Ulrich Hoerni has been involved in nearly every phase of the project, actively supported between 1993 and 1998 by Peter Jung. The executive committee of the Society of Heirs of C. G. Jung released the scripts for publication. At ETH Zurich, the former head of the archives, Beat Glaus, made scripts available and supervised transcriptions. Ida Baumgartner and Silvia Bandel transcribed shorthand notes of the lectures; C. A. Meier provided general information about the lectures; Marie-Louise von Franz provided information about the editing of Barbara Hannah's scripts; Helga Egner and Sonu Shamdasani gave editorial advice; at the Jung Family Archives, Franz Jung and Andreas Jung made scripts and related materials available; at the Archives of the Psychological Club, the former chairman, Alfred Ribi, and the librarian, Gudrun Seel, made lecture notes available; and Sonu Shamdasani found notes taken by Lucie Stutz-Meyer. Rolf Auf der Maur and Leo La Rosa provided legal advice and managed contracts.

In 2004, the Philemon Foundation took on the project, in collaboration with the Society of Heirs of C. G. Jung, and since 2007, with its successor organization, the Foundation of the Works of C. G. Jung, and the ETH Zurich Archives. At the Foundation of the Works of C. G. Jung, Ulrich Hoerni, former president and executive director, Daniel Niehus, president, and Thomas Fischer, executive director, oversaw the project, and Ulrich Hoerni, Thomas Fischer, and Bettina Kaufmann, editorial assistant, reviewed the manuscript. Since 2007, Peter Fritz of the Paul & Peter Fritz Agency has been responsible for managing contracts. At the ETH Zurich Archives, Rudolf Mumenthaler and Michael Gasser, former directors, Christian Huber, director, and Yvonne Voegeli made scripts and related documents available. Nomi Kluger-Nash provided Rivkah Schärf's shorthand notes of some of the lectures, which were then transcribed by Silvia Bandel. Steve Martin provided Bertha Bleuler's shorthand notes of some of the lectures.

The editorial work has been overseen by Sonu Shamdasani, general editor of the Philemon Foundation. Between 2004 and 2011, the preparatory phase of the compilation of the scripts and editorial work was undertaken by Angela Graf-Nold. From 2012 the compilation and editorial work has been undertaken by Ernst Falzeder, Martin Liebscher, and (since December 2018) Christopher Wagner at the Health Humanities Centre and German department at UCL.

The editor and co-translator of this volume, Ernst Falzeder, would like to express his deep gratitude to the board of the Philemon Foundation and in particular to Judith Harris for her invaluable support throughout the work on this project; to Sonu Shamdasani, Martin Liebscher, and Chris Wagner at UCL for the outstanding collaboration, guidance, and help; to Ulrich Hoerni and Thomas Fischer from the Foundation of the Works of C. G. Jung; to the team at Princeton University Press, in particular Fred Appel, Karen Carter, and Jay Boggis; to the members of the Phanês group; to the community of the translators' forum at *https://dict.leo.org/englisch-deutsch/*; and to a great number of friends, relatives, and supporters throughout the years too numerous to be mentioned here, in particular Eva Eckmair, Eva Erhart, Florian Falzeder, Gemmo Kosumi, Gerhard Laber, Martin Liebscher, Tommaso Priviero, Christian Schacht, Sonu Shamdasani, and Hale Usak. Special thanks to Marina Leitner—as always.

Chronology 1933–1941

COMPILED BY ERNST FALZEDER, MARTIN LIEBSCHER, AND SONU SHAMDASANI

Date	Events in Jung's Career	World Events
1933		
January	Jung continues his English seminar on Christiana Morgan's visions, on Wednesday mornings.	
30 January		Hitler is appointed Reich Chancellor in Germany by the president, Paul von Hindenburg.
February	Jung lectures in Germany (Cologne and Essen) on "The Meaning of Psychology for Modern Man" (CW 10).	
27 February		Reichstag fire in Berlin. The fire, possibly a false flag operation, was used as evidence by the Nazis that the Communists were plotting against the German government, and the event is seen as pivotal in the establishment of Nazi Germany. Many arrests of leftists. On 28 February, the most important basic rights of the Weimar republic were suspended.
4 March		"Self-dissolution" of the Austrian parliament, and authoritarian régime under Chancellor Engelbert Dollfuß.
5 March		In the German federal elections, the National Socialists become the strongest party with 43.9 % of the votes.

Date	Events in Jung's Career	World Events
13 March to 6 April	Jung accepts the invitation of Hans Eduard Fierz to accompany him on a cruise on the Mediterranean, including a visit to Palestine.	
18/19 March	Athens. Visits the Parthenon and the theatre of Dionysus.	
23 March		The German parliament passes the *Ermächtigungsgesetz* (Enabling Act), according to which the government is empowered to enact laws without the consent of the parliament or the president of the Reich—a self-disempowerment of the parliament.
25–27 March	Jung and Fierz visit Jerusalem, Bethlehem, and the Dead Sea.	
28–31 March	Egypt, with visits to Gizeh and Luxor.	
March to June		Franklin D. Roosevelt starts the New Deal.
1 April		Nationwide boycott of Jewish shops in Germany.
5 April	Via Corfu and Ragusa the *General von Steuben* lands in Venice, from where Jung and Fierz take the train to Zurich.	
6 April	Ernst Kretschmer resigns from the presidency of the General Medical Society for Psychotherapy (GMSP) in protest against "political influences." Jung, as vice-president, accepts the acting presidency and editorship of the society's journal, the *Zentralblatt für Psychotherapie*.	
7 April		The German parliament passes a law that excludes Jews and dissidents from civil service.

Date	Events in Jung's Career	World Events
22 April		"Non-Aryan" teachers are excluded from their professional organizations, "non-Aryan" and "Marxist" physicians lose their accreditation with the national health insurance.
26 April		Formation of the Gestapo.
1–10 May		Ban on trade unions in Germany.
10 May		Public burning of books in Berlin and other cities, including those of Freud.
14 May	The Berliner *Börsen-Zeitung* publishes "Against psychoanalysis," describing Jung as the reformer of psychotherapy.	
22 May		Sándor Ferenczi dies in Budapest.
27 May/ 1 June		The German government imposes the so-called Thousand Mark Ban, an economic sanction against Austria. German citizens had to pay a fee of 1000 Reichsmark (or the equivalent of about $5,000 in 2015) to enter Austria.
21 June	Jung accepts the presidency of the GMSP.	
26 June	Interview with Jung on Radio Berlin, conducted by Adolf Weizsäcker.	
26 June–1 July	1 July Jung gives the "Berlin Seminar," opened by a lecture by Heinrich Zimmer on 25 June.	
14 July		"Law for the prevention of hereditarily diseased offspring" in Germany, which allows the compulsory sterilization of any citizen with alleged hereditary diseases.
14 July		In Germany, all parties with the exception of the NSDAP are banned or dissolve themselves.

Date	Events in Jung's Career	World Events
August	Jung's first attendance at the Eranos meeting in Ascona, giving a talk "On the Empirical Knowledge of the Individuation Process" (retitled, CW 9/1).	
15 September	Foundation of a new German chapter of the GMSP, whose statutes demand unconditional loyalty to Hitler. Matthias H. Göring, a cousin of Hermann Göring, is named its president.	
22 September		Law on the "Reich chamber of culture" in Germany, enforced conformity [*Gleichschaltung*] of culture in general, tantamount to an occupational ban on Jews and artists who produce "degenerate" art.
7/8 October	Meeting of the Swiss Academy of Medical Science at Prangins. Jung presents a contribution on hallucination (CW 618).	
20 October	Jung's first lecture on "Modern Psychology" at ETH.	
5 December		Repeal of Prohibition in the United States with the passage of the Twenty-first Amendment.
10 December		Nobel Prize in Physics to Erwin Schrödinger and Paul A. M. Dirac "for the discovery of new productive forms of atomic theory."
December	Jung publishes an editorial in the *Zentralblatt* of the GMSP, in which he contrasts "Germanic" with "Jewish" psychology (CW 10). The same issue contains a manifesto of Nazi principles by Matthias Göring that, be it by oversight or on purpose, also appears in the international, not only German, edition, against Jung's wishes. Jung threatens to resign from the presidency, but ultimately stays on.	

Date	Events in Jung's Career	World Events

Other Publications in 1933:
"Crime and Soul," CW 18
"On Psychology," revised version in CW 8
"Brother Klaus," CW 11
Foreword to Esther Harding, *The Way of All Women*, CW 18
Review of Gustav Richard Heyer, *Der Organismus der Seele*, CW 18

1934

Date	Events in Jung's Career	World Events
20 January		German "Work Order Act" and introduction of the "Führer principle" in economy.
12–16 February		Civil war in Austria, resulting in a ban of all social-democratic parties and organizations, mass arrests, and summary executions.
23 February	Jung's last lecture at ETH in the winter semester of 1933/34.	
27 February	Gustav Bally publishes a letter to the editor of the *Neue Zürcher Zeitung* ("Psychotherapy of German Origin?"), in which he strongly criticizes Jung for his alleged Nazi leanings and anti-Semitic views.	
Spring	Beginning of Jung's serious and detailed study of alchemy, assisted by Marie-Louise von Franz.	
13–14 March	Jung publishes a rejoinder to Bally in the *NZZ* ("Contemporary Events", CW 10).	
16 March	Publication of B. Cohen, "Is C. G. Jung 'Conformed'?" in *Israelitisches Wochenblatt für die Schweiz*.	
21 March	Jung's last seminar on Christiana Morgan's visions. The participants opt for continuing the English Wednesday morning seminars with one on Nietzsche's *Zarathustra*.	

Date	Events in Jung's Career	World Events
March/April	C. G. Jung, *The Reality of the Soul: Applications and Advances of Modern Psychology*; with contributions from Hugo Rosenthal, Emma Jung, and W. Müller Kranefeldt.	
April	Jung publishes "Soul and Death" (*CW* 8).	
April	Interview with Jung, "Does the World Stand on the Verge of Spiritual Rebirth?" (*Hearst's International-Cosmopolitan*, New York).	
ca. April	Jung publishes "On the Present Position of Psychotherapy" in the *Zentralblatt* (*CW* 10).	
20 April	Jung's first ETH lecture in the summer semester.	
2 May	Jung starts the English seminar on Nietzsche's *Zarathustra* (until 15 February 1939).	
5 May	Jung's inaugural lecture at ETH, "A General Review of Complex Theory" (*CW* 8).	
10–13 May	Jung presides at the Seventh Congress for Psychotherapy in Bad Nauheim, Germany, organised by the GMSP, and repeats his talk on the complex theory. Foundation of an international umbrella society, the IGMSP, organized in national groups that are free to make their own regulations. On Jung's proposition statutes are passed that (1) provide that no single national society can muster more than 40% of the votes, and (2) allow that individuals (that is, Jews, who are banned from the German society) can join the International Society as "individual members." Jung is confirmed as president and as editor of the *Zentralblatt*.	

Date	Events in Jung's Career	World Events
29 May	James Kirsch, "The Jewish Question in Psychotherapy: A Few Remarks on an Essay by C. G. Jung," in the *Jüdische Rundschau*.	
31 May		The "Barmen Declaration," mainly instigated by Karl Barth, openly repudiates the Nazi ideology. It becomes one of the founding documents of the Confessing Church, the spiritual resistance against National Socialism.
15 June	Erich Neumann, letter to the *Jüdische Rundschau* regarding Kirsch's "The Jewish Question in Psychotherapy."	
30 June/ 1 July		The so-called Röhm putsch. SA leader Ernst Röhm, other high-ranking SA members, and alleged political opponents are executed on Hitler's direct orders, among them Röhm's personal physician Karl-Günther Heimsoth, a longtime member of the IGMSP and a personal acquaintance of Jung.
13 July	Jung's last ETH lecture in the summer semester.	
25 July		Failed putsch attempt by the Nazis in Austria, in which the Austrian chancellor Engelbert Dollfuß is murdered.
29 July		New government in Austria under chancellor Kurt Schuschnigg, who tries to control the Nazi movement by his own authoritarian, right-wing regime.
2 August		Death of Reich president Paul von Hindenburg. Hitler assumes chancellorship and presidency in personal union, as well as supreme command of the Wehrmacht.
3 August	Gerhard Adler, "Is Jung an Antisemite?", in the *Jüdische Rundschau*.	

Date	Events in Jung's Career	World Events
August	Eranos meeting in Ascona. Jung talks on "The Archetypes of the Collective Unconscious" (CW 9/1).	
1–7 October	Jung gives a seminar at the Société de Psychologie in Basle.	
26 October	First ETH lecture of the winter semester 1934/35.	

Other publications in 1934:

With M. H. Göring, "Geheimrat Sommer on his 70th Birthday," *Zentralblatt* VII

Circular letter, *Zentralblatt*, CW 10

Addendum to "Zeitgenössisches," CW 10

Foreword to Carl Ludwig Schleich, *Die Wunder der Seele*, CW 18

Foreword to Gerhard Adler, *Entdeckung der Seele*, CW 18

Review of Hermann Keyserling, *La Révolution Mondiale*, CW 10

1935		
	Jung becomes titular professor at ETH.	
	Jung completes his tower at Bollingen, by adding a courtyard and a loggia.	
19 January	Jung accepts an invitation to lecture in Holland.	
22 January	Foundation of the Swiss chapter of the IGMSP.	
24 February		Swiss extend the period of military training.
1 March		Saarland reunion with Germany, marking the beginning of German expansion under the National Socialists.
8 March	Final ETH lecture of the winter semester 1934/35.	

Date	Events in Jung's Career	World Events
16 March		The German government officially denounces its future adherence to the disarmament clauses of the Versailles Treaty.
26 March		Switzerland bans slanderous criticisms of state institutions in the press.
27–30 March	Eighth Congress of the IGMSP in Bad Nauheim (*CW* 10).	
2 May		Franco-Russian Alliance.
3 May	First ETH lecture of the Summer semester 1935.	
May	Jung attends and lectures at an IGMSP symposium on Psychotherapy in Switzerland.	
5 June		The Swiss government introduces an extensive armament expansion program.
11 June		The disarmament conference in Geneva ends in failure.
28 June	Publication of Jung's contribution at the May IGMSP symposium, "What Is Psychotherapy?", in the *Schweizerische Ärztezeitung für Standesfragen* (*CW* 16).	
12 July	Jung's last ETH lecture in the summer semester.	
August	Eranos lecture on "Dream Symbols of the Individuation Process" (*CW* 9/1).	
15 September		Passing of the so-called Nuremberg Laws in Germany. These laws deprive Jews (defined as all those one-quarter Jewish or more) and other non-"Aryans" of German citizenship, and prohibit sexual relations and marriages between Germans and Jews.

Date	Events in Jung's Career	World Events
30 September– 4 October	Jung gives five lectures at the Institute of Medical Psychology in London, to an audience of around one hundred (CW 18).	
October		Conclusion of the "Long March" in China.
2 October	Publication of Jung's "The Psychology of Dying" (a shortened version of "Soul and Death") in the *Münchner Neueste Nachrichten* (CW 8).	
2–3 October		Italian invasion of Ethiopia.
6 October	Interview with Jung, "Man's immortal mind," *The Observer*.	
15 October	The Dutch national group of the IGMSP retracts their invitation to host its next international congress, because of the events in Nazi Germany. In his answer, Jung states that this "compromises the ultimate purpose of our international association" and declares that he will resign as its president, which he does not carry through, however.	
25 October	First ETH lecture of the Winter semester 1935/36.	
8 November		Switzerland tightens banking secrecy laws (leading to the numbered bank accounts).
December		Nobel Peace Prize for leftist German journalist and editor Carl von Ossietzky. Hitler forbids Germans to accept Nobel Prizes.

Date	Events in Jung's Career	World Events

Other publications in 1935:

The Relations between the I and the Unconscious, 7th edition, CW 7

Introduction and psychological commentary on *The Tibetan Book of the Dead*, CW 11

"Votum C. G. Jung," CW 10

"Editorial" (*Zentralblatt* VIII), CW 10

"Editorial Note" (*Zentralblatt* VIII), CW 10

"Fundamentals of Practical Psychotherapy," CW 16

Foreword to Olga von Koenig-Fachsenfeld, *Wandlungen des Traumproblems von der Romantik bis zur Gegenwart*, CW 18

Foreword to Rose Mehlich, *J. H. Fichtes Seelenlehre und ihre Beziehung zur Gegenwart*, CW 18

1936

Date	Events in Jung's Career	World Events
February	"Yoga and the West" (CW 11).	
February	"Psychological Typology" (CW 6).	
27 February		Death of Iwan Pawlow.
Spring	Formation of the Analytical Psychology Club in New York City.	
March	Jung publishes "Wotan" in the *Neue Schweizer Rundschau* (CW 10).	
6 March	Final ETH lecture of the winter semester 1935/36.	
7 March		German military forces enter the Rhineland, violating the terms of the Treaty of Versailles and the Locarno Treaties. This remilitarization changes the balance of power in Europe from France towards Germany.
28 March		The property of the *Internationaler Psychoanalytischer Verlag*, and all its stock of books and journals, are confiscated.

Date	Events in Jung's Career	World Events
May		Foundation of the *Deutsches Institut für psychologische Forschung und Psychotherapie* in Berlin, headed by M. H. Göring ("Göring Institute"), with working groups of Jungian, Adlerian, and Freudian orientation. Psychoanalysis was tolerated, but on the condition that its terminology be altered.
May	"Concerning the Archetypes, With Special Consideration of the Anima Concept," in the *Zentralblatt* (CW 9/1).	
1 May	First ETH lecture of the summer semester 1936.	
July		Beginning of Spanish civil war.
10 July	Final ETH lecture of the summer semester 1936.	
19 July	Jung and Göring attend a meeting of psychotherapists in Basel, with representatives of different depth-psychological schools (among others, Ernest Jones for the International Psycho-Analytical Association).	
August	Eranos meeting; Jung speaks on "Representations of Redemption in Alchemy" (CW 12).	
1–16 August		Summer Olympics in Berlin. Germans who are Jewish or Roman are virtually barred from participating.
21–30 August	Jung travels on board the *Georgia* from Le Havre to New York City. Upon arrival in New York, he releases a "Press Communiqué on Visiting the United States," setting forth his political—or, as he insisted, his nonpolitical—position.	

Date	Events in Jung's Career	World Events
September	Jung lectures at the Harvard Tercentenary Conference on Arts and Sciences, on "Psychological Factors Determining Human Behavior" (CW 8), and receives an honorary degree. His invitation had given rise to controversy.	
12–15 September	Jung is guest of the Anglican bishop James De Wolf Perry in Providence, Rhode Island, addresses the organization "The American Way," and then leaves for Milton, Mass., where he is guest of G. Stanley Cobb.	
ca. 19 September	Jung starts a seminar on Bailey Island, based on Wolfgang Pauli's dreams.	
2 October	Jung gives a public lecture at the Plaza Hotel in NYC. The talk is privately published by the New York Analytical Psychology Club under the title, "The Concept of the Collective Unconscious" (CW 9/1).	
3 October	Jung leaves New York City.	
4 October	Interview with Jung, "Roosevelt 'Great,' Is Jung's Analysis," New York Times (later published under the title, "The 2,000,000-year-old man").	
14 October	Jung lectures at the Institute of Medical Psychology, London, on "Psychology and National Problems" (CW 18).	
15 October	Interview with Jung, "Why the World Is in a Mess. Dr. Jung Tells Us how Nature Is Changing Modern Woman," Daily Sketch.	
18 October	Interview with Jung, "The Psychology Of Dictatorship," The Observer.	

Date	Events in Jung's Career	World Events
19 October	Jung lectures before the Abernethian Society, St. Bartholomew's Hospital, London, on the concept of the collective unconscious (CW 9/1).	
25 October		Secret peace treaty between Germany and Italy.
27 October	Jung begins his seminars at ETH on children's dreams and old books on dream interpretation.	
3 November		Franklin D. Roosevelt is re-elected for his second term.
25 November		Anti-Comintern Pact between Germany and the Empire of Japan, directed against the Third (Communist) International.
10 December		Abdication of Edward VIII in England.

Other publications in 1936:
Review of Gustav Richard Heyer, *Praktische Seelenheilkunde*, CW 18

1937

3–5 January	Jung participates in the workshop of the Köngener Kreis (1–6 January) in Königsfeld (Black Forest, Germany), on "Grundfragen der Seelenkunde und Seelenführung" [Fundamental Questions of the Study and Guidance of the Soul].	
30 January		Hitler formally withdraws Germany from the Versailles Treaty. This includes Germany no longer making reparation payments. He demands a return of Germany's colonies.
23 April 1937	After a break in the winter semester Jung's ETH lectures commence.	

Date	Events in Jung's Career	World Events
26 April		Germany and Italy are allied with Franco and the fascists in Spain. German and Italian airplanes bomb the city of Guernica, killing more than 1,600.
23 May		Death of John D. Rockefeller.
28 May		Death of Alfred Adler in Aberdeen, Scotland.
9 July	Final ETH lecture of the summer semester 1937.	
19 July		The NS exhibition on "Degenerate art" opens at the Institute of Archaeology, Munich.
August	Eranos Lecture on "The Visions of Zosimos" (CW 13).	
2–4 October	Ninth International Medical Congress for Psychotherapy in Copenhagen, under the presidency of Jung (CW 10).	
October	Jung is invited to Yale University to deliver the fifteenth series of "Lectures on Religion in the Light of Science and Philosophy" under the auspices of the Dwight Harrington Terry Foundation (published as "Psychology and Religion," CW 11).	
	Dream Seminar (continuation from the Bailey Island seminars), Analytical Psychology Club, New York.	
December	Jung is invited by the British Government to take part in the celebrations of the 25th anniversary of the founding of the Indian Science Congress Association at the University of Calcutta. He is accompanied by Harold Fowler McCormick Jr. (1898–1973) and travels through India for three months.	

Date	Events in Jung's Career	World Events
13 December		Nanjing falls to the Japanese. In the six weeks to follow, the Japanese troops commit war crimes against the civilian population known as the Nanjing Massacre.
17 December	Arrives in Bombay by P & O Cathay.	
19 December	Jung reaches Hyderabad, where he is bestowed an Honorary Doctor Degree by Osmania University in Hyderabad; night train to Aurangabad.	
20 December	Aurangabad: visits the Kailash Temple at Ellora, and Daulatabad.	
21 December	Visits the caves at Ajanta.	
22 December	Sanchi, Bhopal, visits the Great Stupa.	
23 December	Taj Mahal, Agra.	
27 December	Benares; Jung visits Sarnath.	
28 December	Jung is awarded the D. Litt. (Doctor of Letters) Honoris Causa by the Benares Hindu University; presentation at the Philosophy Department: "Fundamental Conceptions Of Analytical Psychology"; guest of Swiss interpreter of Indian Art Alice Boner; visits the Vishvanatha Śiva Temple.	
29 December	Calcutta.	
31 December	Jung travels to Darjeeling.	

Other publications in 1937:

"On the Psychological Diagnosis of Facts: The Fact Experiment in the Näf Court Case," CW 2

Date	Events in Jung's Career	World Events
1938		
1 January	Three-hour conversation with Rimpotche Lingdam Gomchen at the Bhutia Busty monastery.	
3 January	Opening of the 25th anniversary of the founding of the Indian Science Congress Association at the University of Calcutta.	
	Jung is treated in the hospital in Calcutta.	
7 January	Jung is awarded (in absentia) the degree of Doctor of Law (Honoris Causa) by the University of Calcutta.	
10 January	Lecture at the College of Science, University of Calcutta: "Archetypes of the collective unconscious."	
11 January	Lecture at the Ashutosh College, University of Calcutta: "The Conceptions of Analytical Psychology."	
13 January	Visits the Temple of Konark ("Black Pagoda").	
21 January	Visits the Chennakesava Temple (also called the Kesava temple) and the temple of Somanathapur (Mysore).	
26 January	Jung in Trivandrum; lecture at the University of Travancore: "The Collective Unconscious."	
27 January	University of Travancore: "Historical Developments of the Idea of the Unconscious."	
28 January	Ferry to Ceylon.	
29 January	Colombo.	

Date	Events in Jung's Career	World Events
30 January	Train to Kandy.	
1 February	Return to Colombo.	
2 February	Embarks on the S.S. *Korfu* to return to Europe.	
12 March		Annexation of Austria by Nazi Germany.
27 April		Edmund Husserl, the founding philosopher of phenomenology, dies in Freiburg, Germany.
29 April	After his return from India, Jung's ETH lecture series recommences.	
May		The League of Nations acknowledges the neutral status of Switzerland.
4 June		Sigmund Freud leaves Vienna; after a stop in Paris, he arrives in London two days later.
8 July	Final ETH lecture of the summer semester 1938.	
29 July–2 August	Tenth International Medical Congress for Psychotherapy in Balliol College, Oxford, under the presidency of Jung; honorary doctorate from the University of Oxford; "Presidential Address" (*CW* 10).	
August	Eranos Lecture on "Psychological Aspects of the Mother Archetype" (*CW* 9/1).	
29 September		Munich Pact permits Nazi Germany the immediate occupation of the Sudetenland.
		Agreement between Switzerland and Germany concerning the stamping of German Jewish passports with "J."
28 October	First ETH lecture of the winter semester 1938/39.	

Date	Events in Jung's Career	World Events
October	Jung's ETH seminar series on the psychological interpretation of children's dreams commences in the winter term of 1938/39.	
9 November		A Swiss theology student, Maurice Bavaud, fails to assassinate Hitler at a Nazi parade in Munich and is guillotined.
9/10 November		Pogrom against Jews in Nazi Germany ("Crystal Night").
23 November	Jung gives his witness statement at the retrial of the murder case of Hans Näf.	

Other publications in 1938:

With Richard Wilhelm, *The Secret of the Golden Flower*, 2nd edition, CW 13

"On the *Rosarium Philosophorum*," CW 18

Foreword to Gertrud Gilli, *Der dunkle Bruder*, CW 18

1939

January 1939	"Diagnosing the dictators," interview with H. R. Knickerbocker, *Hearst's International-Cosmopolitan*.	
15 February	The last of Jung's seminars on Nietzsche's *Zarathustra* and hence of Jung's regular English-language seminars.	
3 March	Final ETH lecture of the winter semester 1938/39.	
28 March		Madrid surrenders to the Nationalists; Franco declares victory on 1 April.
April	Visits the west country in England in connection with Emma Jung's Grail research.	
4 April	Lecture at the Royal Society of Medicine in London, "On the Psychogenesis of Schizophrenia" (CW 3).	

Date	Events in Jung's Career	World Events
5 April	Lecture at the Guild of Pastoral Psychology, London, on "The Symbolic Life."	
28 April	First ETH lecture of the summer semester 1939.	
May	Surendranath Dasgupta lectures on Patañjali's *Yoga Sûtras* in the Psychology Club, Zurich.	
	Interview with Howard Philp, "Jung Diagnoses the Dictators," *Psychologist*.	
July	At a meeting of delegates of the International General Medical Society for Psychotherapy Jung offers his resignation.	
7 July	Final lecture of the summer semester 1939.	
August	Eranos Lecture on "Concerning Rebirth" (CW 9/1).	
1 September		Nazi German troops invade Poland; Britain and France declare war on Germany two days later, beginning World War II.
		Switzerland proclaims neutrality.
23 September		Sigmund Freud dies in London at the age of 83.
	Moves his family for safety to Saanen in the Bernese Oberland.	
1 October	Jung's obituary of Freud is published in the *Sonntagsblatt der Basler Nachrichten* (CW 15).	
3 October	First ETH lecture of the winter semester 1939/40.	

Date	Events in Jung's Career	World Events
October	Jung's ETH seminar series on the psychological interpretation of children's dreams commences in the winter term 1939/40.	

Other publications in 1939:
"Consciousness, Unconscious and Individuation," CW 9/1
"The Dreamlike World of India" and "What India Can Teach Us," CW 10
Foreword to Daisetz Teitaro Suzuki's *Introduction to Zen-Buddhism*, CW 10

1940

Date	Events in Jung's Career	World Events
8 March	Final ETH lecture of the winter semester 1939/40.	
9 April		German troops invade Norway and Denmark.
10 May		German invasion of Belgium, the Netherlands, and Luxembourg.
12 May		France is invaded by Germany.
14 June		German troops occupy Paris.
20 June	In a letter to Matthias Göring, Jung offers his resignation of the presidency of the International General Medical Society for Psychotherapy.	
12 July	Jung sends his final letter of resignation to M. Göring.	
19 July		Hermann Göring is appointed Reichsmarschall.
August	Eranos lecture on "A psychological approach to the dogma of the trinity" (CW 11).	
7 September (–21 May 1941)		German aerial raids against London ("the Blitz").

Date	Events in Jung's Career	World Events
29 October	Jung's ETH seminar series on children's dreams commences in the winter semester 1940/41.	
8 November	First ETH lecture of the winter semester 1940/41.	

Other publications in 1940:

Foreword to Jolande Jacobi, *Die Psychologie von C. G. Jung*, CW 18

1941

13 January		Death of James Joyce in Zurich.
28 February	Final lecture of the winter semester 1940/41.	
2 May	First ETH lecture of the summer semester 1941.	
11 July	Jung's final ETH lecture.	
August	Eranos lecture on "Transformation Symbolism in the Mass" (CW 11).	
7 September	Presents a lecture on "Paracelsus as a Doctor" to the Swiss Society for the History of Medicine in Basel (CW 15).	
5 October	Presents a lecture on "Paracelsus as a Spiritual Phenomenon" in Einsiedeln, on the 400th anniversary of the death of Paracelsus (CW 13).	

Other publications in 1941:

Essays on a Science of Mythology. The Myth of the Divine Child and the Mysteries of Eleusis, together with Karl Kerényi, CW 9/1
"Return to the Simple Life," CW 18

Introduction to Volume 2

ERNST FALZEDER

WHEN JUNG STARTED lecturing for his second semester at ETH Zurich, on 20 April 1934, he had a full workload amid the turbulent times in the world surrounding him.[15] Apart from his clinical practice, and the time he devoted to the preparation and delivery of these lectures, he ended the *Visions* seminar on 21 March 1934 (Jung, 1977) and a few weeks later, on 2 May 1934, started a new seminar on Nietzsche's *Zarathustra* (Jung, 1988). He had also become engaged in the Eranos meetings in Ascona, organized by Olga Fröbe-Kapteyn. He had given a talk at its first meeting, in August 1933 (Jung, 1933a), and would do so at its second meeting the following year. In general, these years were marked by his turn to the intense study of alchemy (see below), as he embarked on a new area of investigation that occupied more and more of his time.

In addition, he published, in 1934, *The Reality of the Soul: Applications and Advances of Modern Psychology*, an anthology with contributions from Hugo Rosenthal, Emma Jung, and W. M. Kranefeldt (Jung et al., 1934), and a number of smaller texts, including his rejoinder to Gustav Bally (Bally, 1934; Jung, 1934e); "The state of psychotherapy today" (Jung, 1934a); "The soul and death" (Jung, 1934c); "Archetypes of the collective unconscious" (his Eranos lecture; Jung, 1934d); and a number of greetings, forewords and afterwords, and reviews.

Hardly anything of these activities, however, is reflected in the lectures. Instead of sharing his interests at the time with his audience, he went back to his beginnings.[16] As he had already pointed out at the beginning of the first semester, any questions addressed to him (which were to be sent to

---

[15] For a chronology, juxtaposing world events and events in Jung's life and career, see Volume 1 (Jung, 2018, pp. lv–lxxvi).

[16] On 5 May 1934, he gave his inaugural lecture at ETH, which also dealt with the complex theory (Jung, 1934b).

him through the post) should be strictly "within the scope of these lectures, rather than broaching the future of European currencies, for instance, or the prospects of National Socialism, etc." (Jung, 2018, p. 2). He wanted to present himself as an "objective" university professor, limiting himself to psychology and its history *sensu stricto*. He had, in the first semester, given an overview of the field and presented various theories and systems of thought in a historical survey, as well as discussing in detail two historic case histories, thus setting the background for his own views, and situating himself in a line of pre-eminent thinkers over the centuries. He was now ready to cautiously move toward an elucidation of his own theories, which he did by retracing his own steps in developing them.

He was in his late fifties, and would turn fifty-nine on 26 July. He had long since gained an independent standpoint vis-à-vis the theories of his erstwhile teachers and mentors, such as Théodore Flournoy, Pierre Janet, Eugen Bleuler, and Sigmund Freud. In an "Address on the occasion of the founding of the C. G. Jung Institute," on 24 April 1948, Jung gave a succinct summary of his own development (1948, § 1130):

> As you know, it is nearly fifty years since I began my work as a psychiatrist. . . . Freud and Janet had just begun to lay the foundations of methodology and clinical observation, and Flournoy in Geneva had made his contribution to the art of psychological biography. . . . With the help of Wundt's association experiment, I was trying to evaluate the peculiarities of neurotic states of mind . . . my purpose was to investigate what appeared to be the most subjective and most complicated psychic process of all, namely, the associative reaction. . . . This work led directly to a new question, namely the problem of *attitude*. . . . From these researches there emerged a *psychological typology* . . . and four function-types. . . . From the beginning . . . [this] went hand in hand with an investigation of unconscious processes. This led, about 1912, to the actual discovery of the *collective unconscious*. . . . This expansion found expression in the collaboration with the sinologist Richard Wilhelm and the indologist Heinrich Zimmer.

In short, he had extensively and intensively traveled both the inner and outer worlds. Starting from humble origins, he had become a world-renowned, if highly controversial, figure, scientifically as well as politically. And now, after having resigned from his lectureship at the University of Zurich in 1913 as a *Privatdocent*, he was reentering the world of academia, and would shortly become a full university professor at ETH in 1935.

One can say that he had arrived at the zenith of his career. His old rival and erstwhile friend, Sigmund Freud, still cast a long shadow, however. Although Jung had secured the highest academic position, had gathered a large international followership around him, had developed an all-encompassing psychological theory that was much talked about, had become a sought-after interview partner in international media, had acquired friends and donors among the famous, rich, and mighty in finance, politics, nobility, academia and science, literature and the arts, and had become a household name in many circles all over the world—still his name was often mentioned only in connection with Freud. Even today, as Sonu Shamdasani observed, Freud and Jung are the two "names that most people first think of in connection with psychology" (in Jung, 2009, p. 193). More often than not they were not named as equals, however, but Jung was portrayed as Freud's former disciple and follower, as someone, like Alfred Adler (who often completed the trio), who had further developed Freud's theory and method, and was either praised or criticized for it, but was still perceived as coming second after Freud, the "original" innovator who had opened up a whole new field of psychological investigation and treatment.[17] The number of his followers, the "Jungians," never surpassed a quarter of the membership of Freud's International Psycho-Analytical Association (IPA), and they were also much more loosely and less effectively organized (cf. Falzeder, 2012).

This was especially so in Germany, where Jung for obvious reasons also wanted to create a strong foothold and not be eclipsed by Freud and the Freudians. As he still wrote in a letter of 1932, even if with a bit of coquettish understatement: "I am just beginning to get known in German speaking countries" (1972, p. 151). Or even, in 1933: "as a matter of fact, there are only few people who have realized that I am saying something other than Freud. Unfortunately, I am unknown in Germany. . . . I also want to correct the impression that I emerged from Freud's school" (ibid., p. 161). It was his conviction, however, that the development of psychotherapy in Germany would be decisive for its future in general. Shortly before the start of the term, on 28 March 1934, he wrote to Max Guggenheim: "Freud once told me quite accurately: 'The fate of psychotherapy will be decided in Germany.' At first it was absolutely doomed, because

---

[17] I am speaking of the *perception* of many, then and now, regardless of whether or not the claim to Freud's originality holds up.

it was regarded as completely Jewish. This prejudice I have stopped through my intervention" (ibid., p. 203).

But even if Jung was successful in gaining some ground among psychotherapists in Germany, and had also succeeded in having bylaws passed that individual members of the International General Medical Society for Psychotherapy (IGMSP)—that is, German Jews who were banned from membership in the German chapter of the IGMSP by the Nazis—could become individual members, this affected primarily the practical psychotherapeutic application of analytical psychology. The members of the IGMSP, as psychotherapists, were mostly practicing medical doctors, and only a few of them did important theoretical work or had ties to academia. Here, at ETH, in his new role as a university professor, he faced a different challenge.

Freud had been appointed *Professor extraordinarius* at the University of Vienna in 1902. This was a merely nominal title, but apart from giving prestige and being bound to attract patients, it also gave him the right to give lectures. After having lectured there for thirty years, he gave his last lecture series in the winter terms of 1915/1916 and 1916/1917, which were then published in 1917 under the title *Introductory Lectures on Psycho-Analysis* (Freud, 1916–1917). This became "Freud's most popular book." Writing in 1955, Ernest Jones listed "five German editions, in addition to several pocket ones issued. . . . It was translated into sixteen languages. . . . There have been five English editions and two American ones" (Jones, 1955, p. 218).

In March 1932, Freud began writing a new series of his *Introductory Lectures*, which appeared in book form on 6 December 1932 (Freud, 1933; Freud and Eitingon, 2004, p. 841). These were actually not held at the university, and were written mainly to help the floundering Internationaler Psychoanalytischer Verlag, to which he donated his royalties. These *Lectures* did, however, keep the dialogue format and continued the numbering of the previous *Lectures*. Both sets of lectures were not specifically addressed to analysts but to the, now imagined, "multitude of educated people" (ibid., p. 6), and presented to them "what novelties, and what improvements it may be, the intervening time has introduced into psycho-analysis" (ibid., p. 7).

Jung was well aware of this and had indeed obtained a copy of the *New Introductory Lectures*. How did he himself try to address "the multitude of educated people," his own wider audience? What were his own "Introductory Lectures on Analytical Psychology"? He had all but completed his own mature theoretical edifice. Nearly all the elements were there: theory of complexes, the collective unconscious and the archetypes, persona, shadow, anima/animus, the self, individuation, symbology, circumambulation, enantiodromia, dream theory, typology and the four functions, active imagination ("transcendent function"), and so forth, and the germs of synchronicity (see, e.g., pp. 20–30). After having found in 1928, through Wilhelm, what he thought was an independent confirmation (outside the field of psychiatry) of his views and experiences, he took up the comparative study of Eastern texts, first in collaboration with Jakob Hauer and Heinrich Zimmer (cf. Jung, 1996; in prep. [1933]). And after having identified the *Secret of the Golden Flower* as an "alchemical treatise," he embarked on his immersion into alchemy and the *mysterium coniunctionis*: "it was the text of the *Golden Flower* that first put me on the right track. For in medieval alchemy we have the long-sought connecting link between Gnosis and the processes of the collective unconscious that can be observed in modern man" (Jung, 1938, p. 4). And indeed he spent the rest of his life studying the psychology of Western alchemy and Christian symbolism. Barbara Hannah dates the beginning of his serious study of alchemy to the spring of 1934. It was at this time that he engaged Marie-Louise von Franz as a research assistant to work on alchemy, as his Greek and Latin were rusty (Hannah, 1976, p. 229).

On 2 November 1928, he was invited by Carl Murchison, editor of a series of overviews on the "psychologies" for each year, published by Clark University, to contribute a chapter on his own psychology for the 1930 volume (ETH Archives). Jung knew of the series and had mentioned it at the beginning of the previous term as an example of the "incredible chaos of opinions" in the field (2018, p. 1) and again at the start of this, the next semester, in similar terms (p. 1). At the time, in 1928, Jung declined to contribute, and suggested Helton Godwin ("Peter") Baynes instead.[18] In the end, no chapter on Jung was included. The section on "analytical psychologies" (Murchison, 1930; part XI) contained three articles: by Pierre Janet on his *analyse psychologique*, by John C. Flugel on (Freudian) psychoanalysis, and by Alfred Adler on individual psychology. Jung's name was mentioned only four times, twice in connection with his association experiments (ibid., pp. 47, 386) and twice in passing in conjunction with Freud and/or Adler (ibid., pp. 32, 461).[19]

In contrast to Freud, Jung was very much at ease and willing to speak in public. He was quite comfortable in giving interviews for newspapers,

---

[18] On Baynes, see Baynes Jansen (2003).
[19] Freud's name appeared thirty-two times.

journals, radio, and eventually TV; he gave public talks and university lectures, held seminars, and enjoyed talking to opinion leaders and politicians. In fact, "Jung could never, or only when he was physically weakened, resist whenever a journalist asked him to give an interview" (Jaffé, 1968, p. 132; my trans.). In the early and mid-1930s, and in addition to his ETH lectures, he gave a number of basic, partly overlapping overviews of his theory in different settings. Apart from various single presentations, he lectured for a week each in Basel, Switzerland (1–6 October 1934) (Jung, 1935 [1934]) and in Ammersfoort, Netherlands (April 1935), on "Basic concepts and methods of analytical psychology," and from 30 September to 4 October 1935 he delivered the well-known Tavistock Lectures (Jung, 1936 [1935]).[20] The by far most detailed, accessible, and inclusive account, however, he presented at the university. This can be viewed as an attempt not only to take stock and review the path he himself had taken but also to meet and challenge Freud by presenting his own version of depth psychology in an academic setting and by establishing a foothold as a professor in academic psychology and psychiatry.

In the previous semester, at the restart of his lectureship at the university, Jung had taken great pains to present himself as a scientist aligning himself with a great number of prestigious thinkers over the centuries, and trying to confront his audience with simple but at the same time strange and peculiar facts, taken from famous historic case histories. This approach had not been an unqualified success, however. Many listeners, especially the younger ones, had been disappointed that the topics Jung addressed in great detail were not the ones they had come to hear him speak about. "There are quite a number of reactions from younger members of the audience," said Jung at the beginning of his ninth lecture on 15 December 1933, "that have confirmed my worst fears. I would have spoken over the top of their heads, and they could not imagine for which reasons I have discussed at length such a curious case as that of the Seeress, which evidently dates from the last century!" (2018, p. 71). This probably referred to some reactions of students, gathered and summarized by a participant named Otto (ETH Archives; undated). They concurred that the lectures did not meet their expectations, specifically, that the topics had been too far-fetched and historical, and that Jung would not talk about contemporary problems and his own psychological theory. Jung again mentioned similar complaints four lectures later: "I have received a

---

[20] Much of the material from Basel and Tavistock was incorporated by Roland Cahen in his edition of Jung's *L'homme à la découverte de son âme* (Jung, 1944).

few reactions, probably from some of the younger members of the audience, wishing me to present fewer case histories, and instead give you more of my own point of view . . . but you must bear in mind that I set out to give a course of lectures on modern psychology, and I cannot claim that modern psychology is identical with myself" (ibid., p. 106).

Perhaps also as a reaction to this feedback, in the second semester Jung did talk much more about his own method and theory. He did this by sharing with his audience the path he himself had taken; *nota bene*, not by recounting his experiences of recording and assessing what he had encountered in his own inner world, but by dealing with experiments and concepts that had earned him scientific renown, beginning with his association experiments, and how he himself discovered "the" unconscious, eventually leading up to various methods of getting to know its contents, in particular, dream analysis.

What Jung did *not* do, for the time being, was to enter into a discussion of the theoretical and methodological differences between his own views and those of Freud (or Adler). Indeed, he did not even mention the name of Freud *at all* in this particular semester, which in itself seems to be a conspicuous omission, since without doubt Freud played a crucial role in the very development he was describing. With hindsight, however, we can see this as a strategy to prepare his audience for a detailed discussion of and comparison with those differences later on, which he did indeed undertake in the following terms. Now that we can see what he was leading up to, we can also appreciate how much an underlying, but still implicit, rivalry with Freud was behind this. As this will become much clearer in the third volume of this series (forthcoming), a commentary on their different approaches and Jung's way of presenting them will be reserved until we consider Jung's specific lectures on this issue. However, here I already want to point out the underlying rationale of Jung's strategy, in which—besides other motives—the long shadow that Freud still cast seems indeed to have played a major role.[21]

Jung began his first lecture by saying, "In my experience, it was in general the basic terms which caused difficulty. I have therefore decided to discuss simpler matters this semester, namely basic terms and methods,

---

[21] Shortly before the beginning of this term, in December 1933, Jung had written a laudatory review of Gerhard Adler's book, *Entdeckung der Seele* [*The Discovery of the Soul*], subtitled *From Sigmund Freud and Alfred Adler to C. G. Jung* (1934 [1933]), which addresses precisely those differences. Jung mentioned this book in his fourth lecture as "a very good description of the functions in the context of so-called typology," but not in the context of Freud or Adler.

with the help of which I hope to explain to you how the notions with which I work came into being."

The first question he addressed is a seemingly simple one: What is psychology? This leads to further questions: What is the present state of psychology? What is its subject? How subjective is it, and how objective can it be? Jung was a dedicated psychologist, and what he mentioned in the seventh lecture could be taken as a motto for his whole enterprise: "[T]he human being is the noblest task of science, towering above all its other tasks. It is the highest and most interesting task, in my unauthoritative opinion." This is reminiscent of Nietzsche, who had demanded "that psychology again be recognized as queen of the sciences, and that the rest of the sciences exist to serve and prepare for it" (1886 [2002], p. 24). It seemed to be more than a rhetorical question when Jung had asked, in 1930, will "Nietzsche be proved right in the end with his 'scientia ancilla psychologiae' [science is the handmaid of psychology]?" (Jung, 1930a, Introduction).

"Psychology is . . . first of all about what is valid in general," he stated, notwithstanding one's own "psychology," but it is also subjective; it is about what occurs to us directly. Its subject is "what is called the soul," *das was man Seele nennt*. And not only is "everything we experience psychic" but "*everything* was once psychic, there is nothing that had not been psychic before, such as the fantasy of an artist or an engineer. Take a railway bridge, or a work of art—or indeed this lectern. Everything that we learn and experience is at first psychic. The only thing that is immediately given and perceptible is something psychic, that is, a psychic image. This is the first and only basis of experience. 'I sense [*empfinde*]' is the first truth." Thus, psychology is both a general phenomenon and something subjective, an almost personal matter. Jung stressed, however, that it was not an arbitrary matter but rather "a phenomenology, a symptomatology."

This led him to the question of how the various views of psychology in its history, which he had presented in the first semester, had been generated, and later to account for national differences in ideas and outlook, in particular to reflect on the question of language, social and religious convictions, institutions, and geographical differences (soil, climate) in general, and on the different characteristics and difficulties of the English, French, and German languages when it came to expressing psychological materials in particular. "Psychology is . . . dealing with a great number of facts," he noted. "But it is extremely difficult to accept these facts as they really are." Once we do accept these facts, there arises the next difficulty, that is, the *representation* of the material, which is a great difficulty indeed: "[I]t is almost impossible to faithfully convey the facts of the matter."

"[T]he fundamental psychological truths can never be couched in delineated terms," because "the sharper a psychological term, the less it designates." Therefore we would have "to learn the art of coming up with terms that are quite general and indeterminate, and yet are still able to convey something." We always have to bear in mind that we are dealing with the totality of a person. It is no use "to isolate a psychic process" for the purpose of study, because then we will have "killed the psychic life in that process."

"There is nothing simple in the psyche." The psyche that reacts to something simple is never simple itself. Each of us perceives differently, so how do we construct a fact or evidence? And how do we faithfully convey the facts we experience? For example, "what do I mean when I assert: 'I'm feeling fine'"? An external observer might register something we are unaware of. "The difficulties arising in this connection were among the reasons," according to Jung, "that led to the recognition of the unconscious as an interfering factor." This gave Jung the opening to enter into a discussion of the concepts of consciousness and the unconscious, and their respective characteristics, which he illustrated with various examples, whether from everyday life, from his clinical experience, from his travels, from the literature, or, quite frequently, from what he still called "primitives."

He described the conscious and unconscious states alternately, stressing their difference but also their interdependence and interrelationship. Consciousness, for instance, "needs an effort, demands energy and work, and thus tires us." It is also "very limited" and "very narrow[,] and excludes a good many ideas." The unconscious, on the other hand, "is present at all times" and "the primordial condition of mankind." "The unconscious is always dreaming." It is also always "active at work, and I am completely dependent on this work." "[C]onsciousness swims on the unconscious world like a round disc, or is like a small island in the ocean. Consciousness can never be identical with the soul, it is only a part, perhaps a very small part, of the soul. The soul is the whole." "Consciousness is to all intents and purposes an organ, an eye or an ear of the soul." The unconscious, on the other hand, "has a fabulous memory. There are things we never knew, so to speak, but that existed nonetheless" and had a discernible effect on us.[22]

---

[22] In this context, Jung came close to Freud's concept of *Nachträglichkeit*, saying, for example: "Often things occurred at a time when our consciousness was still unable to realize their value. We were perhaps conscious of them but we were unaware of their value."

Having introduced this basic differentiation between consciousness and the unconscious, he then proceeded to discuss consciousness as a "perceptual" or "orientation organ," and "those functions of consciousness that serve our orientation toward the inside," or the "inner sphere." Leaving aside his distinction between introverted and extraverted types for the time being, he introduced the well-known four functions that, according to Jung, guide this orientation—sensation, thinking, feeling, and intuition—and, as always in these lectures, illustrated them and how they are "curiously interrelated" with the help of many examples. We also hear more about his distinctions between rational and irrational functions, and developed (superior) and underdeveloped (inferior) functions. Sensation tells us what a thing *is*, thinking what it *means*, feeling how we *valuate* it, and intuition gives us "the invisible aura that surrounds the thing," something best rendered as *Ahnung* (presentiment, premonition, inkling, hunch, foreboding). "In effect, the latter is an excellent term while 'intuition' allows for many different meanings." It is a "function of perception by unconscious means." The intuitive "does not look at things, but sees," and simultaneously has "a truly remarkable capacity for non-observation." Foreshadowing his concept of synchronicity, Jung spoke about the "law of the series" and the "laws of coincidence." "Since intuitions are never completely conscious, intuition is a strange borderline function . . . that is never really tangible, and we know as much of it as we do of the fourth dimension. Therefore, my definition of intuition is somewhat makeshift, and in fact a declaration of scientific bankruptcy." In fact, we find here

---

However, those things "were registered as important by the unconscious, and . . . may reemerge later." Freud's term for this later effect of earlier impressions is the notoriously difficult-to-translate *Nachträglichkeit*, which has been rendered as "deferred action" in English and "après-coup" in French. As Laplanche and Pontalis (1967, p. 111) define the term: "experiences, impressions and memory-traces may be revised at a later date to fit in with fresh experiences or with the attainment of a new stage of development. They may in that event be endowed not only with a new meaning but also with psychical effectiveness." Roudinesco and Plon (2006, p. 57) specify that this is particularly true for traumatic events, which "take on significance for a subject only *après-coup*, that is, within a later historical and subjective context that gives them a new significance. This term sums up the ensemble of the Freudian conception of temporality, according to which a subject constitutes their past in reconstructing it as a function of the future or of a project" (my trans.).—Be it that he was unaware of the parallels, or be it that he wanted to avoid drawing attention to them, Jung in general did not credit Freud in these lectures with substantial contributions that he shared with or had taken over from him (see also pp. 7–8 and note 39 on the antithetical meaning of primal words) but stressed the differences between them or, in particular, used Freud as a "case history" that displayed certain peculiarities, as toward the end of the first semester (2018, p. 130): "we would have to conclude that his thinking came only out of his complexes. Now, we will refrain from assuming as much, we are much too polite for that."

probably the most detailed and simultaneously most accessible discussion of the intuitive function in Jung's work.

At the center of the functions there is the "I," and all functions relate to it. The I usually has a main thought and a large number of secondary thoughts that it keeps to itself, "for otherwise there would be no individuality." "These secondary thoughts make the I the keeper of the great seal of all secrets."

Although functions are subject to the will and can be directed, they can occur involuntarily in consciousness or can also proceed unconsciously. This unconscious course of our functions "is . . . a very comforting fact. For it allows us to expect with some certainty that what we do not think, perceive, and intuit with our consciousness, will be done for us by the unconscious."

Jung stressed that these "functions were not discovered by myself, I only stumbled on this treasure trove, for the functions are an ancient fact." "In Lamaism, this theory of functions is developed to a significant extent. There, it is called 'mandala.'"

All of this is a reformulation of views he had already expounded elsewhere, most famously in *Psychological Types* (1921), but here in layman's terms and in an easily accessible form, and as such already a valuable addition to the Jungian oeuvre, or even, with only slight exaggeration, a *Jung for Beginners* by the man himself. In addition, however, we also find bits and pieces, snippets and asides, which may open up new perspectives. For instance, he introduced still another "function" that is particularly characteristic of consciousness and "a distinct cultural phenomenon": "the function of the volitional faculty [*Funktion des Willensvermögens*], in short, the *will*. If it were on a par with the other functions, we might call it a fifth function, but it is better to see it as a superordinate, central function of the I. It reflects the fact that a certain amount of energy is freely available in consciousness, like a mobile division or reserve unit. This psychically available energy stands at the disposal of consciousness."

Jung then turned to a more detailed discussion of the so-called unconscious, personal and collective. "Unconscious" simply means "that which we do not know." "It is not even possible to prove that these things exist when they are in the unconscious, for the essential character of the latter is that it is unknown." The unconscious is thus "a negative boundary term, one which indicates: it is dark there. We have no knowledge of what actually happens there. We postulate, however, that the things of which we are not conscious at this moment somehow nevertheless exist." As to his distinction between personal and collective unconscious, he stated that there is "nothing mythical about it, for it is really a very practical idea."

"The unconscious evidently comprises psychic processes that have either already become lost to consciousness and become forgotten, or ones that do not yet exist and have not yet been born." "What emerges from the personal unconscious is 'my business'; what emerges from the collective unconscious are matters related to humanity in general and therefore not my business in this sense." "[T]heir personal aspect is only a metaphor." Filling a lacuna in his earlier accounts, he gave a detailed map of the differentiation and stratification of its contents, in particular as regards cultural and so-called racial differences.

There follows an exposition of methods for rendering accessible the contents of the unconscious. From early on, Jung had looked for additional methods to do so, apart from the "only rule that psychoanalysis lays down in this respect is: let the patient talk about anything that comes into his head," because, apart from conscious resistances, the patient's "not talking to the point [*danebenreden*] does not prove that the patient is *consciously* concealing certain painful contents; it can also occur quite unconsciously." In these cases, "the analyst has to resort to other measures. One of these is the association experiment. . . . A second expedient is the analysis of dreams; this is the real instrument of psychoanalysis" (1913, §§ 531–533). And this is exactly what Jung did in these lectures, giving a detailed exposition of these measures.

Thus, he first turned to the association experiment and the psychogalvanic method, with many examples, including their use for *Tatbestandsdiagnostik* or diagnosis of evidence in forensics, or how a detailed account of the study of associations in families enables the psychic structure of families, the *spiritus familiaris*, to be revealed. All of this is further evidence, by the way, of how important these researches remained to him, and how useful he continued to find them for didactic purposes.

"The main finding" of these experiments was "the insight into the existence of complexes." "Complexes have to be taken seriously, they have dynamic energy, they live in our psyche, and they seem to be bad things, yet it is these very complexes which lead us to our fate." Or: "Complexes are so to speak our family ghosts." And: "For the complex has the unpleasant characteristic that one forever does what tempts one, thereby inducing a kind of vicious circle." It is possible, however, that "complexes can be made to disappear by taking certain provisions . . . through atonement or a confession, either by the patient resuming a reasonable life style, or through reintegration into the community." "There is still another way of ridding oneself of a complex, namely by getting into some kind of continuity that commits the same sin."

Gradually, however, Jung came to realize that a quasi-objective measure of complexes, with the stopwatch in hand, as it were, is not possible. The subject's response depends on what they think this is about and on who is asking. A sobering and embarrassing experience for Jung must have been his expert opinion in the trial of one Hans Näf in November 1934, accused of murdering his wife,[23] in which Jung concluded, on the basis of the *Tatbestandsdiagnostik* arrived at through the association experiment he had conducted with him, that "the subject's psychological situation, as revealed by the experiment, in no way corresponds to what one would empirically expect in an innocent person" (Jung, 1937 [1934], § 1388). Näf was found guilty and sentenced to lifelong imprisonment. Jung even used this case, in an interview with the *Daily Mail* in 1935, as evidence for the soundness of his method. A retrial in 1938 revealed, however, that Näf was in fact innocent of the charges and resulted in his acquittal. The fact that the experiment was not an objective measure surely contributed to Jung's turning away from it—although he continued, as here, to use it for didactic purposes—and instead to concentrate on psychological analysis.

The semester—and the book—concludes with an overview of the topic of dreams and the study of several of them. It "occurred to me early on that dreams are simply complexes." Both represent "an invasion of the unconscious." Dreams "are actually like association experiments turned inside out. In these experiments, we have stimulus words that strike the complex and elicit it to emerge, whereas dreams themselves produce the test words. . . . If you emphasize these words and certain motifs that often recur in dreams, it is really revealing when you ask: 'What comes to your mind about this?'"

This is reminiscent of Freud's method of free association, but with one crucial difference. Whereas the Freudian analysand is asked to associate on and on, to "go off on a tangent," string-wise, as it were, from A to B, from B to C, from C to D, and so on, in the expectation that the associations will ultimately lead to the *hidden* meaning of the dream, a postulated X, which had been *distorted* and rendered unintelligible by the mechanisms of censorship and dream-work, Jung started out by using "controlled association." The dreamer is asked to approach the motifs and images of a dream in a circumambulatory manner, so to speak, and not to lose sight of them, because they are not distortions or "compromise

---

[23] The following information is based on research by Martin Liebscher (in Jung & Neumann, 2015, pp. 81–82).

formations" of opposed forces within the psyche. According to Jung, dreams are "spontaneous products of the unconscious soul. They are pure nature, and therefore convey an unadulterated, natural truth." They represent a "communication or message of the unconscious, of the all-one soul of humankind" (Jung, 1933b, §§ 317–318; my trans.). "But nature is not, in herself, a guide," as he noted elsewhere, "for she is not there for man's sake. Ships are not guided by the phenomenon of magnetism. We have to make the compass a guide." Thus, products of the unconscious, such as dreams, have to be used "with the necessary conscious correction that has to be applied to every natural phenomenon in order to make it serve our purpose" (1918, § 34).

The "compass" he gave to his listeners sounds simple enough: "A dream should always be written down at once, otherwise we inevitably lie to ourselves. It is best to note it down on a sheet of paper that one divides into three columns: The first column is for the text; the second is for the context, that is, comments on the keyword and associations we have to it, as if this were a complex word. In the third column we can note the interpretation. This is the way to work on a dream humbly, by oneself, when there is no accomplished analyst at hand to do it for one."

The deciphering of dreams, and reading and accepting the message from the unconscious, however, is not just a party game. The lectures break off with the analysis of one particular dream, the interpretation of which "did not enlighten the dreamer. He learned nothing from it and refused to accept my explanation of this dream. So, unfortunately, he went on following his ambitions and a disastrous situation followed." Obviously, there was more to be said on the topic, and so Jung started the following, third semester (forthcoming) by saying: "Those of you who attended last summer's lectures will remember that they dealt with methods for revealing the inside of the human psyche. We spoke of the word association method, combined with breathing, of the psycho-galvanic method, and finally of dream analysis. This semester we will proceed along the same path and study the psychology of dreams. The investigation of the inner psyche is a practical possibility for doctors; it is the investigation of the unknown motive. Just to know that a thing exists is not enough, one must know what it is and all about it. The human psyche is the most important object of all."

It is to this quest that Jung devoted his lifelong work—the sum total of which up to that point he was now ready to convey to a general audience of "educated people" in these lectures at a prestigious university. Welcome to what could be called his own *Introductory Lectures to Analytical Psychology*.

Consciousness and the Unconscious

Lecture 1

20 April 1934

In my experience,[24] it was in general the basic terms that caused difficulty. I have therefore decided to discuss simpler matters this semester—namely basic terms and methods—with the help of which I hope to explain to you how the notions with which I work came into being.

In psychology, we enter an incredibly vast and controversial field. It thus differs from other sciences, whose boundaries are more or less sharply delineated. The field known as psychology is completely unbounded, and one might even call it vague and nebulous. One very significant fact in this respect is that each year an American university publishes a thick volume entitled *Psychologies of the Year so-and-so*, for instance of 1932 or of 1933. Each year there is an array of "psychologies."[25] If one has traveled about the world a bit, and has seen various people, nations, and universities, one gains the impression that psychology consists of the sum of individual declarations of faith rather than of a system. Now each such declaration wants to exclude the others and to be the only one to tell the universally valid truth. As understandable as such a wish is, sometimes, however, such convictions are exaggerated.

In psychology, after all, very many personal views exist, precisely because there is an infinite number of aspects. For instance, people usually tend to consider psychology a personal matter. One *has* a certain psychology, a certain disposition, that is to say one loves this or hates that, and so on. Psychology is, however, first of all about what is valid in general. It deals with what is known as the psyche or soul. Everything that is made and done by man ultimately goes back to this. *Everything* was once

---

[24] That is, in the previous semester (Jung, 2018).
[25] Jung here repeats a point he had also made at the start of the first semester (see 2018, p. 1 and note 58). The series was edited by Carl Murchison and published by Clark University Press, Worcester, MA. The first traceable volume is from 1925 (Murchison, 1925).

psychic, there is nothing that had not been psychic before, such as the fantasy of an artist or an engineer. Take a railway bridge, or a work of art—or indeed this lectern.

Everything that we learn and experience is at first psychic. The only thing that is immediately given and perceptible is something psychic, that is, a psychic image. This is the first and only basis of experience. "I sense [*empfinde*]" is the first truth. Reality—that is, what we call real—is the reality of our sensation. In the very first instance, sensation is what is real and what conveys to us the character of reality in the first place.

There is, of course, an outer world, that is to say, things that exist beyond the psyche. I would obviously not go so far as to claim a solipsism that looks upon everything as psychic.[26] And yet everything we experience is psychic. If, for instance, you see light, then this is something psychic, for there is no light "in itself," nor is there sound. They exist merely in the brain, and what they look like there we do not know. We only have knowledge of a complicated process of which we are unconscious. In fact, we need complex apparatuses to determine what that thing is which has sounded in our head or blinded our eyes.

Psychology is thus the science of that which occurs directly. Everything else is given to us only indirectly. When you burn yourself, for instance, by touching a hot iron, this process is by no means simple but highly complicated. Our nerves must be affected, etc., for an impression to register in our brain that we call pain. What this pain looks like one level further down, that is, when it is still located in the nerve, eludes us completely. Little wonder, then, that psychology touches upon a range of other sciences: pedagogics, medicine, philosophy, history, ethnology, mysticism, art, the philosophy of religion, and so on, and also parapsychology.

Consequently, misunderstandings and prejudices are not only possible but happen all the time. Since the psyche is an immediate given, we all believe that it is the given per se. We must work a great deal on ourselves to realize that our own experience of the psyche is not *the* general experience.

Some attempt to restrict psychology, because such a broadness of the concept strikes them as uncanny. Sometimes psychology is therefore confined to the theory of attention, volition, consciousness, or affects—serving to explain, for instance, why people love and hate each other, why they are abnormal or normal, or how one might be successful, and so on. Medical

---

[26] Solipsism: a theory in philosophy that one's own existence is the only thing that is real or that can be known with certainty.

psychology, too, is as a rule limited to the psychology of neuroses, and consequently its validity is also limited. But psychology is first and foremost a general phenomenon, because the psyche is first and foremost a general, given fact.

Here, however, I must at once draw your attention to a paradoxical fact. Although the psyche is in the first instance a general phenomenon, it is, on the other hand, a most personal matter. The individual is the living unity, for there is no other life than individual life. So it would of course be possible to also posit: Psychology is what is given individually. This is an antinomy, but in psychology we cannot advance unless we learn the very difficult art of paradoxical thinking.

First and foremost, psychology finds expression in language, in social and religious convictions, and in institutions. We are highly dependent on the language in which we speak. One could almost identify language with the psyche. We thus depend on language as much as on moral or religious preconditions—and not merely on those that we share. There are unspoken preconditions we are not at all conscious of, which we might even oppose, and which nonetheless influence us, above all our milieu and our psychic heredity; in addition, there are social, political, geographical, and ethnological preconditions. Indeed, the soil and the climate influence not only the psyche but even our anatomy, or, to say the least, our behavior.

This can be seen primarily by observing the children of Europeans born on foreign soil, for instance, in the colonies. This is such a universal fact that English children born in the colonies are called "colonials," meaning that something is "not right" with them. Under some circumstances, these influences can utterly dominate an individual. This, of course, is an imponderability.

I remember, for instance, a family with seven children in New York. One of these children was born in Frankfurt am Main,[27] a true German girl who could be spotted as such fifty meters off. Four children had been born in New York and were undoubtedly American. Should you ask me, however, how I could detect the difference, I could not tell you what "an American ought to look like." Another example: a picture published in a German newspaper, depicting American politicians who had been appointed Indian chieftains. "Now who is the Indian?" Or, one evening, I came past a large factory in Buffalo. I had no idea, I said, that there were really so many Indians in this area! No way, I was told by an American

---

[27] Thus in Sidler. Hannah: "seven children four of whom had been born in Hamburg [sic]" (p. 94). This anecdote is missing in Schärf.

4 · LECTURE I

doctor, not a drop of native American Indian blood in them, they are all descendants of Czechs, Poles, Germans, Italians, etc. But the habitus has a very distinct character, which is quite unmistakable. If this escapes a psychologist, I would suggest appointing a sales assistant of a large department store as chair of psychology, for such matters are of course those that matter. Imagine treating an Englishman as if he were French! Vice versa, would you greet a Frenchman with "Hello boy"?[28]

Professor Boas has measured the skulls of immigrants and of their children at Columbia University in New York. He found out that the shapes of their skulls had changed in the direction of the Yankee type.[29] Now if even the body changes, you can imagine that naturally the soul does, too, as I observed in the case of colonials.[30] All immigrants to the colonies are as a rule in a very strange state, known as "going black," that is, they have turned black under the skin. When I was in Central Africa, I observed myself and my dreams very closely in order to discover when the first black mark appeared on me, other than those I already had. . . . [31] With some experience you can tell when someone has turned black. When you enter the house of such a man you will immediately notice that the tablecloth has marks, the crockery is chipped and broken, pictures are hanging askew, and that he feels quite palpably uncomfortable—like a lion walking to and fro in his cage. Nor will the man be able to look you straight in the eye; he will squint, look around nervously, and he will

---

[28] This expression in English in the notes.

[29] Slightly different versions of the anecdotes about the workers in Buffalo and the family of German immigrants in New York, as well as a report on Boas's investigations, can also be found in Jung's "The complications of American psychology" (1930b, §§ 948–949).—Jung had met Franz Boas (1858–1942), one of the fathers of modern anthropology, in 1909 at the twentieth anniversary of Clark University in Worcester, where Boas, together with Jung and Freud, had been among the invited lecturers (cf. Skues, 2012). From his investigations between 1908 and 1910 on the bodily form of descendants of immigrants, he concluded that "American-born descendants of immigrants differ in type from their foreign-born parents" (Boas, 1912, p. 60). On Boas and Jung, see Shamdasani (2003, pp. 276–278).

[30] Sidler has the following quote here, obviously something Jung said he was told: "Why for God's sake do you want to study the psychology of these Niggers [sic], because they haven't any. Study ours, that's much more interesting."

[31] At the end of his stay in North Africa in 1920, Jung had a dream that was, to him, "the first hint of 'going black under the skin,' a spiritual peril which threatens the uprooted European in Africa to an extent not fully appreciated," an "archetypal experience." The dream expressed the conflict between Jung's "feeling superior because I was reminded at every step of my European nature" and "the existence of unconscious forces within myself which would take the part of these strangers" (Jung, 1962, pp. 273–274). Cf. Jung, 1930b, §§ 962, 967; 1931 [1927], § 97.

already have that same strange rolling motion of the eyes as the Negroes. Negroes can't look you in the face, probably for fear of the evil eye. We are giving them the evil eye because *we* are able to stare at somebody, and that is why the Europeans are of ill repute, because it is only their medicine men who can do this.

I waited for a long time,[32] without noticing a thing, until I was in the bush for the first time, in complete wilderness, "1,000 miles from anywhere."[33] Two of us Europeans went for a walk. I was carrying a new elephant gun and my companion was armed with a heavy Colt, and thus we went "botanizing." I soon had a strange feeling that something was amiss with my eyes, so I cleaned the lenses of my spectacles. I observed myself closely and concluded that my eyes were blinking. I could not find any organic cause, but every time my eyes looked around the blinking set in again. I then established the theory that my eyes were evidently looking for something. I somewhat doubted this theory, however, until someone else confirmed it. Another friend, an American, went out to shoot guinea fowl. The area was covered in termite hills. As he was walking along, he overlooked a seven-foot green mamba, a kind of cobra, one of the few snakes that attacks human beings at night, and was almost killed by it.[34] The snake had been lying in the sun on top of a termite hill. The sun was beating down, which is when they get particularly vicious. It had actually intended to go for the Negro, but he had noticed. Now if the American's eyes had also flickered then he, too, would have taken note of the snake. This has to do with prevailing local conditions in this strange country, where one must have one's eyes everywhere at all times. Thus, characteristic influences arise from such conditions. There are, of course, also other things that can prompt these effects.

One of the most common prejudices against psychology is that it is a kind of cookery book providing recipes for how one should do things. There's a picture in an American magazine, showing a mother who took

---

[32] That is, for signs in himself of "going black."
[33] This expression in English in the notes.
[34] This happened to George Beckwith, who had accompanied Jung, together with Helton Godwin "Peter" Baynes and Ruth Bailey, on the so-called Bugishu Psychological Expedition. In "Archaic man," Jung related the events of that day: "I nearly stepped on a puff-adder, and only managed to jump away just in time. That afternoon my companion returned from a hunt, deathly pale and trembling in every limb. He had narrowly escaped being bitten by a seven-foot mamba which darted at him from behind a termite hill. He would undoubtedly have been killed had he not been able to wound the brute with a shot at the last moment. At nine o'clock that night our camp was attacked by a pack of ravenous hyenas. . . . Such a day gave our Negroes food for thought" (1931 [1930], § 125).

her child on her knee in order to punish it and had to hold it there while she found the right place in her book on education in order to see what to do next! Psychology is not an arbitrary matter, however, but a phenomenology, a symptomatology, dealing with a great number of facts. But it is extremely difficult to accept these facts as they really are, because so many facts in psychology are outright tantalizing, so that we think, "This shouldn't be like this! This should be different!" because we ourselves are directly affected, and most often arrive at a quite incorrect judgment. Thus, immediately at our first encounter with such matters we form certain judgments.

A further difficulty in psychology is the representation of its material. Often we have to describe certain facts or events and must resort to ordinary, everyday language to do so. The resulting picture may satisfy ourselves, but not the person to whom we are telling it. In fact, one should actually tell everyone certain facts in *his own language*.[35] Otherwise one can never be certain that one has been correctly understood. As it is, things appear differently to each and every person.

Our language is incredibly deficient in describing psychological nuances. French, for example, is not suited for psychology, since it has very clear terms and concepts, but it is ideally suited for jurisprudence, since it leaves no holes unplugged. In psychology, however, many holes remain open, indeed, must remain open so that the necessary understanding can be reached. English is better suited, particularly those words deriving from Anglo-Saxon. The German language is very good; it is still so little developed and unspecific, even though the Germans are said to be the nation of poets and thinkers. So German is not a good language for philosophy, but it is excellent for psychology, even though the Germans are very poor psychologists, as their political history proves. The Chinese written language is probably best suited to our purpose because it still has signs and hieroglyphs, and because you can attribute your special meaning to each sign. This can be seen best in the translations of Laotse King;[36] the

---

[35] Again, Hannah differs slightly: "One should really describe every single one of these facts in its *own* language" (p. 95).

[36] *Sic* in Sidler, missing in Hannah; obviously a condensation of the name of Lao Tze, an ancient Chinese sage whose identity has not been securely established, and the *Tao te Ching*, of which he is traditionally regarded as the author or compiler and which describes the *Tao* as the source and ideal of all existence and advocates the state of *wu wei*, literally "non-action" or "not acting." Jung described the latter as "the non-action of the Chinese, which is not a non-action" (1972, p. 305).

hieroglyphs are so versatile that any number of things can be discerned from them.

I mention this since in psychology we encounter a difficulty that recently also struck an Englishman.[37] The fundamental psychological truths can never be couched in sharply delineated terms. A fitting psychological term is entirely indeterminate, but it is just capable of conveying something important. The sharper a psychological term, the less it designates; consequently, it is also much more off the mark since nothing in the psyche is simple. Every psychological entity is always a highly complicated, very complex matter. Nothing psychic can be isolated. If you seem to have been able to isolate a psychic process, rest assured that you have killed the psychic life in that process.

Now we could simply strike our colors and say that nothing can be done about psychology anyway. But this is not the case; it's just that the task is especially difficult. We need to learn the art of coming up with terms that are quite general and indeterminate, and yet can still convey something. This peculiar complexity of psychic matters can be seen in language itself, in words such as "courage"; "water"; or "good, better, best." You have no idea of the manifold connotations these words carry. "Good, better, best"[38]—this seems so simple, and yet each of these words looks back on a long, possibly millennia-old history. They contain the primordial words that continue to resonate. There is so much that resonates in this comparative: "good"—"better." "Better" derives from "bad," Old High German *bat* or *bass*, meaning "good" (as in *fürbass gehen*, to stride, to advance vigorously). In Anglo-Saxon, its meaning keeled over into the opposite. And this still resonates, so that when we utter the word "good" and also sincerely mean it, the word still comes tinged with a slight doubt. Very often the history of a word secretly contains its opposite meaning, and if this fails to somehow resonate, the term or concept is incomplete, just like a muscle that acts in opposition to the specific movement generated by the agonistic muscle: When you stretch or bend your arm, you must at the same time innervate the opposite muscle. The same applies to

---

[37] Sidler then notes, in quotation marks, the beginning of a passage that Jung obviously quoted from that unnamed source, but the notes then break off in the middle of the second phrase, obviously because he could no longer follow what Jung said. Here, the essence of the quote is given without quotation marks. The source of the reference could not be identified.

[38] The second time Jung quotes this comparative and superlative, he does so in English.

the notion of a given word, which also secretly contains its contrary meaning.[39]

For instance, no educated Frenchman can speak of *Pucelle d'Orléans*[40] without thinking that *pucelle* also means "whore." He cannot, however, recall that *pucelle*, from Italian *pucella*, originally meant "small flea." These are *enantiodromatic* transformations. The term *enantiodromia* comes from our old friend Heraclitus[41] and means "to run counter to one another," "to run into one's opposite": thus, cold into hot, hot into cold, high into low, low into high. This law of enantiodromia plays a particularly significant role in psychology.

The German *Seele* and the English "soul" have a strange etymology. They derive from Proto-Germanic *seivalo* and Gothic *seivala*. These are etymologically linked to the related Greek word *aios*, "to shine in glaring colors." Aiolos, or Aeolus in Latin, the mighty mover, is the Greek God of the winds. Now this word has all but vanished in the word "soul," and only Old Slavonic still has a related word.[42]

The Greek word for wind in the New Testament is *pneuma*. In Arabic, the wind also has the meaning of spirit. German *Geist* derives from *ufgeistia*, Swiss-German *ufgeisten*, to be aroused or moved, to be bewildered, utterly fascinated, thus in a highly aroused emotional state. It is similar in the miracle of Pentecost:[43] There came a rushing mighty wind, like a geyser, and people believed the disciples were inebriated because they spoke in foreign tongues; hence, a geyser-like violent eruption of wind.

In the ancient legend, Aiolos is described as a God who sits on a mountain-like island and holds an instrument shaped like a lance. There

---

[39] Jung does not mention it here, but in 1910—at the height of their collaboration and friendship—Freud had published an article, "The antithetical meaning of primal words," in which he had drawn attention precisely to this "existence of contradictory primal meanings" of words (1910, p. 159), partly using the same examples as Jung, e.g., "Our '*bös*' ('bad') is matched by a word '*bass*' ('good')" (ibid.).

[40] The Maid or Virgin of Orléans: that is, Joan of Arc.

[41] Jung repeatedly credited Heraclitus with coining this term. Although the concept is in fact in accordance with the latter's philosophy, the term itself was not used by Heraclitus in the extant texts but first turned up in a later summary of his philosophy by Diogenes Laërtius.

[42] The authoritative *Deutsches Wörterbuch* by Jacob and Wilhelm Grimm (1854–1960) states that neither the word's origin nor its relatedness to other words is clear (*von noch nicht aufgeklärter Herkunft und Verwandtschaft*). Contemporary etymology links *Seele*, Old High German *se(u)la*, Gothic *saiwala*, English "soul," with *See* (lake), meaning "the one who belongs to the lake." In Germanic mythology, the souls of the unborn and the dead dwelt in the water (*Duden, Herkunftswörterbuch der deutschen Sprache*).

[43] Acts 2.

is a cave in the mountain, in which the winds are captured. From time to time he pokes the mountain with his lance, and so releases an evil wind. Precisely this is *ufgeisten*, that is, to cast into a state of enthusiasm and excitement. The God who rules this state is Aiolos, the God of the soul. The soul is the phenomenon that arises from keeping these evil wind powers within.

If you ever travel to Verona and visit the cathedral, you will see a saying in Latin that reads: *In patientia vestra possidebitis animas vestras*—"In your patience you will possess your souls."[44]

---

[44] Luke 21, 19 (KJV).—Jung had visited Verona in October 1910 during a bicycle trip through Northern Italy with his friend Wolfgang Stockmayer (see Freud & Jung, 1974, p. 359).

Lecture 2

27 April 1934

There is nothing simple in the psyche. There are said to be "simple" tests, but I assure you that no such thing exists. In the association experiment, for example, the questions are simple enough, but not the answers of the psyche. Easy as the test can be seen to be, it still comes up against a complicated psyche. The psyche that reacts to a test is not "simple," and it responds to an experiment in an unpredictable manner. The test subject might appear to be much more stupid than he really is, for example. For it is the entire soul that reacts, and the entire soul is incredibly complicated. We have no idea what will come to light.

I could hang a red square on the wall, for instance. Everyone will see the same object, and everyone will agree it is red. But even though everyone is sure that it appears exactly the same to everybody else, we all see some individual variant of it. We all perceive it in a highly specific and characteristic manner, of which we may not be aware ourselves. This leads us to a further difficulty, the construction of facts or evidence. We have only language at our disposal to accomplish this task, or possibly images. If we probe deeper into a particular experiment, however, we will see that everyone sees matters in a particular way. King Ludwig of Bavaria[45] commissioned a number of artists to paint the same motif in the garden of Tivoli near Rome. Each artist painted it according to his overall perception. The results were exceedingly varied. To outsiders some of the pictures seemed to be very far from reality, for not only the object but the subject of the artist appeared in them. The same occurred in a journalistic seminar on experiments on witness reports. Some incident was

---

[45] Probably not Ludwig II (1845–1886), the highly eccentric "Swan King" who commissioned, among others, the construction of the fantastic Neuschwanstein Castle, but Ludwig I (1776–1868), who reigned from 1825 to 1848 and was known for his patronage of the arts.

staged, and the students were instructed to report on the facts of the matter.[46]

Where not external but psychic processes are concerned, however, it is almost impossible to faithfully convey the facts of the matter. Our ability to report on psychic facts is extremely limited; for instance, what do I mean when I assert: "I'm feeling fine"? Such a limitation constitutes a large obstacle. The difficulties arising in this connection were among the reasons that led to the recognition of the unconscious as an interfering factor. Something unconscious can enter everywhere without our being aware of it, although an external observer might be able to register it. Apart from consciousness there exists an indeterminably large area of unconscious processes, which can enter at any given moment, without our having an inkling.

This unconscious is present at all times, not only when something special occurs. It is at any rate much more untiringly alive than consciousness. We spend one-third of our lives in sleep—that is, in an unconscious state—while we spend the remaining two-thirds only more or less conscious. As you know, there are people who are properly awake only after ten o'clock in the morning; others do not come to life until after four p.m., and then perhaps only for a mere two hours. Consciousness needs effort, demands energy and work, and so it tires us out. Consequently, we lapse into a certain dream state whenever we can or when nothing is going on. Some people can still observe their thoughts while in this state, but most people cannot.

This is the primordial condition of mankind. Primitives spend the largest part of their lives in this state. They sit around and "dream." We assume they are thinking, but far from it! One primitive was most upset when I asked him what he was thinking about, because he believed that a person who is quiet and then engages in thought is mad.[47] In reality, however, all kinds of things are happening inside him in this twilight state, although he is not aware of this. The unconscious is constantly dreaming. At this very moment, for instance, while we are all listening to this lecture, we are all simultaneously dreaming, each of us dreaming his own dream, but each of us in the dark and below the threshold.

---

[46] In the beginning of his scientific career, Jung wrote several papers on the psychological diagnosis of facts or events, based on his association experiments (Jung, 1905a, 1905b, 1908, 1910 [1909]; cf. Jung, 1937 [1934]).

[47] In the previous semester, Jung had told the same anecdote thus: "When one primitive adopted a position like Rodin's 'Thinker,' he was asked, 'What are you thinking about?' He jumped up furiously, and exclaimed, 'But I am not thinking at all!'" (2018, p. 96).

I could, for instance, make a slip of the tongue or a certain word might not occur to me. This is a symptom of my consciousness gliding over a depth in the unconscious while I was speaking. If I focused my consciousness on this, I could observe the event and then tell you about it. Doing so, however, requires a certain training, and not everyone can do this. An incredible array of things that I know are present at each moment, but they are excluded from consciousness. They are unconscious, and, from the viewpoint of consciousness, they are in a sleeping state. In reality the unconscious is not sleeping at all, but is actively at work. In fact, I am completely dependent on this work of the unconscious and the fact that it puts the words I need in my mouth. If it ceased collaborating, we would all be shamefaced because our minds would go blank. What crosses our minds or "occurs" to us[48] comes from the unconscious.

Our consciousness is thus very limited. It is narrow and cannot deal with many things at the same time. Total clarity of contents is possible only in a state of focused consciousness. The more focused consciousness is, the smaller is the number of its objects. When it relaxes somewhat, the number of its contents may increase, but they will no longer be as distinct. When there are very many such objects in consciousness, it will become flattened, and its representations will be leveled out. The manic state, a flattening of representations, is the chief symptom of a certain mental illness, characterized by an incredible flood of ideas and associations, which can seldom be observed in normal persons.

So as a rule normal consciousness is very narrow and excludes a good many ideas. These must be present somewhere, however. They exist in a latent state, but can still be reproduced and accessed. Thus we are unconscious of many things that concern us directly at a given moment, for instance, the posture of our body, how we walk or sit, the gestures we make with our hands, our facial expression, and a whole range of actions, such as automatic actions. You are walking down a street, people are coming your way, and you step to one side. And by the time you reach the end of the street you don't know for how many people you have stepped aside. You look at your watch, but you don't realize what time it is. Just give it a try and ask someone who has just glanced at their watch what time it is. They will immediately pull out their watch again.[49] Then there

---

[48] In German, the equivalent of "an idea crosses my mind / occurs to me" is: *eine Idee fällt mir ein* oder *ich habe einen Einfall*, literally: an idea falls into me / invades me; I have an invasion.

[49] Jung had already given this as an example of unconscious perception in the second lecture of the first semester (2018, p. 11).

are things that slip our minds "because they are better left unheard and unseen." Other contents can be reproduced only indirectly. That is, they slipped from consciousness and were so thoroughly forgotten that I cannot reach them by an act of will. We might then say, "Let me sleep on it." But indirect automatic recall is also possible.

Let me illustrate this. A man is out for a walk and goes past a farm. When he has passed the farm—he has already gone ahead for several hundred yards—he realizes that he is being flooded with very vivid childhood memories. He then remembers that he has just walked past a farm, and he is suddenly overcome by the distinct smell of a goose-pen. Now, as a matter of fact, his entire childhood was soaked, as it were, in the smell of a goose-pen. But did his consciousness know this? No, not at all. These contents had been evoked unconsciously. They had arisen indirectly, after a few minutes, triggered by the smell.

Finally, there are also contents, or ideas, that never arise and that cannot be reproduced. This must be taken as a metaphor, however, as "something I never thought of." If we conceive of the soul as consisting of consciousness and unconsciousness, we may also talk about unconscious contents. Thus there are things, and a considerable number, too, that have occurred in our lives and of which we have no knowledge. No one can claim to know his own life story; we know only a very small part of it. Often things occurred at a time when our consciousness was still unable to realize their value. We were perhaps conscious of them, but we were unaware of their value. The unconscious seems to have a very well-developed sense of the value of things. There are many things that escaped consciousness, but were registered as important by the unconscious, and that may re-emerge later. These facts are significant insofar as what someone has experienced is not irrelevant—not consciously experienced—that would be an experience proper, but what has in fact affected him in his entire psyche. It is absolutely impossible to go through life events without being affected.

Take two men, for instance. One of them has read a thousand books, the other none. The first, however, has forgotten what he has read in those thousand books, but he will still be a different person from the non-reader, and you will be able to immediately identify him because the unconscious will have registered the fact.

It has been established that the unconscious has a fabulous memory. There are things we never knew, so to speak, but that existed nonetheless. Somnambulistic persons, for instance, can unconsciously register everything they experience. This can be proven by hypnosis. I remember a woman who was admitted to the Burghölzli in a somnambulistic state. She had torn off all her clothes and was completely naked, wrapped in a blanket, when she was brought by the police. She had forgotten everything from the moment when she had fallen ill and had been admitted. I hypnotized her, and asked her: "At what time were you admitted?"

"At eight o'clock sharp."

So she was completely oriented.

A famous case of such an *automatisme ambulatoire* was published by Forel.[50] A gentleman of a well-reputed family was sitting in a coffee house reading a newspaper report of a Mister X who had disappeared in Australia. He pondered the matter and finally concluded that he himself was this very person. After all, he had been in Australia. He consulted Forel and declared himself mad. Forel placed him under hypnosis and elicited the facts one by one. He had been stricken with dengue fever in Australia, and had slipped into an unconscious state, in which he purchased a passage on a ship. The other people on board only noticed that he was withdrawn and taciturn, and that he read a lot. In this twilight state, he traveled to Zurich and then read about his case in the newspaper. "Such cases occur almost exclusively in France," Forel observes. "It seems that the German genus is less theatrically inclined." Such textbook cases are rare, however.

I recall the case of a nineteen-year-old girl, diagnosed as schizophrenic, who had already spent a year and a half at the clinic. I discovered, however, that the entire symptomatology of this case consisted in the patient's listening inward all the time, with such concentration that she could pay no attention to the outer world. She had dilated pupils, like all such cases. If one succeeded, however, in capturing her attention for an instant, her pupils changed. This encouraged me. Her consciousness was located where we have dreams, and vice versa. This filled her with tension. It occurred to me that a drama might be unfolding inside her, and I finally worked it out: It was an exciting story that she had experienced on the moon. There is a strange relationship between the moon and mental illness, by the way.

---

[50] The case was indeed Forel's, but it was written up and published by Forel's student Max Naef (1897). Jung had already quoted it in his doctoral thesis (1902, § 17). Auguste Forel (1848–1931), Eugen Bleuler's predecessor as head of the Burghölzli clinic and professor of psychiatry at the University of Zurich, was an eminent Swiss psychiatrist and neuro-anatomist, and also a noted myrmecologist. He is also known for his early contributions to sexology and psychology. He was a pioneer of "psychotherapy" and was pivotal in introducing hypnotism and hypnotic suggestion in Switzerland. As a result of his experiences in psychiatry, he become an ardent spokesman of the temperance movement, banning alcohol in his clinic, a tradition taken over by Bleuler.

We speak of "lunatics,"⁵¹ that is, persons affected with "lunacy." So I asked the patient: "Why can't you just tell me this story? Why must I try so terribly hard to get it out of you?" "Because," she said, "the story was never—in words!"⁵²

There is, after all, psychic thinking beyond consciousness, and it is exhausting to put it in words. These are internal dramas, which cannot be brought into consciousness by a conscious effort. They can be reached only through special training or hypnosis.

Kant speaks of the realm of "obscure representations," which would occupy half a world.⁵³ If we now compare this unconscious world with our world of consciousness, we see that consciousness swims on the unconscious world like a round disc, or is like a small island in the ocean. Consciousness can never be identical with the soul; it is only a part, perhaps a very small part, of the soul. The soul is the whole. If you want the whole person, you must always wait for the unconscious to speak as well. With consciousness, you only get a person's more or less good intentions. It was therefore a very good rule among students that one had to first fall prey to some decent intoxication to see which personality emerged, which is interesting indeed. Personality alters in a conspicuous manner. All kinds of things then come to light, which might hardly entice you to have dealings with that person—or, in fact, just the opposite!

Consciousness is to all intents and purposes an organ, an eye or an ear of the soul. It is localized in the brain—although we can't be entirely certain about this, since consciousness takes strange leaps. When I once discussed this with a Pueblo Indian chieftain, I was somewhat embarrassed and at the moment wished I had a somewhat more elephant-like skin—for the white man does not look at all attractive in the consciousness of the underdog. "The Americans are all mad," he told me. "They believe one thinks up there, but of course one thinks with the heart!"⁵⁴ Later the Negroes told me that one thinks with the stomach.

We find it touching when someone says he thinks with the heart. But if people come and tell us they think with their stomach, this is really not

---

⁵¹ In English in the notes.
⁵² More details on this case can be found in Jung, 1958, § 571.
⁵³ See Jung, 2018, pp. 10, 12–13, and note 82.
⁵⁴ Jung repeatedly referred to this encounter with Ochwiay Biano ("Mountain Lake") (cf. 1962, p. 276), and had in fact also talked about it, in a slightly different version, in the first semester: "[He] said to me: 'Americans are mad! They say that we think with our heads. But only madmen think with their minds; reasonable people think with their stomachs!" (2018, p. 45).

very poetic. They have this impression because they actually think only when something affects their intestines. On the level of the Pueblo Indians, it is what quickens their heartbeat or makes their heart jump that causes them to think. What goes on in their heads does not count, because only sick people think with the head! Now if you think only what quickens or slows down the heart, or indeed makes it stand still, then you are on the Pueblo level. They think only the awful or the sublime; that is, everything but the ordinary. Matters become even more incomprehensible to us with the Negroes. What we live thinkingly, they live utterly unconsciously. What makes them think is fright, anger, or the sublime, the numinous, the mighty, everything that "upsets their stomach," what causes jaundice or abdominal pain. We believe they have no sense of nature, but the primitive reacts very emotionally to the beauty of nature.

I was once sitting with the son of a chief. There was a humming noise: "It is good and beautiful." The primitives thus perceive such matters, but they must already have acquired a significant emotional force, or else they will not reach their consciousness. This is still lying dormant, and therefore they cannot think logically—they *act* logically.

This is because consciousness, insofar as it is identical with the brain, is actually a sense organ, because the brain has ectodermal filiation. The central nervous system develops in the embryo through the infolding of the exterior skin, which probably also explains the merely perceptual character of consciousness. It is therefore perfectly logical if earlier psychology sought to derive consciousness from sensations. Condillac, for instance, asserted that all consciousness ensues from sensation, and unconsciousness from consciousness.[55]

---

[55] Jung had already introduced the French philosopher Étienne Bonnot de Condillac (1715–1780) and his principal work, *Traité des sensations* (1754 [1798]), in the first semester: "Condillac learned that all psychic life originates in sensation. . . . [T]he whole of the soul is empty. The mind would be an absolute *tabula rasa*" (2018, p. 20). Jung, of course, repeatedly refuted this, as also below, in the fifth lecture: "For the mind is neither a *tabula rasa* nor a blank slate. We make the great mistake of thinking that children are born as a *tabula rasa*, but this is not the case" (p. 39).

Lecture 3

4 May 1934

CONSCIOUSNESS IS NOT a universal condition but rather a structured organism. We can distinguish different functions of consciousness. Even though all these functions form an almost inseparable absolute continuum, one or the other function can be separated, at least conceptually. In essence, consciousness is a perceptual organ, one could also say, an orientation organ: that is, an organ whose sensory portals link it to the inner world, and which conveys the outside to the inside, and vice versa. Because the inside is not empty, as little as the outside.

Let us now consider those functions of consciousness that serve our orientation toward the inside. Let us call the inside the "inner sphere"; the "outer sphere" will then correspond to the visible world. The first function that we come across is the *sensation* function. It serves the perception of what is given by the senses. The senses form organs through which the outer world enters the psyche. The psyche is an intricate organ, which perceives and registers the stimuli fed to the senses.

By definition, perception as such contains only sensations: that is, nothing other than the stimulus that the object has triggered in the sense organ and that is conveyed to the brain and to consciousness. Here we are, of course, drawing an artificial line, by segregating sensation from the psychic continuum. In reality, however, we are completely unable to perceive something like a "pure" sensation. For as soon as the sensory stimulus enters consciousness, it is accompanied by a psychic content that does not originate in the sensory sources but exists *a priori*, that is, prior to the sensory stimulus. Therefore, pure sensation exists only in theory. In general, sensation is first followed by a kind of primitive *thinking*, namely, the question of what the sensory stimulus could mean. In practical experience, this is linked to the sensory perception as such. It is as if our eyes had already told us what the object is. In reality, however, our eyes provide only a visual image, but they say nothing about what the actual thing is. We only notice this if we see something and have absolutely no idea of what it is. It is a thinking function that tells us what it is. Confronted with the unknown we begin to think, and then become aware of the fact that we are thinking. By its nature, thinking is a psychic function that is associated only very indirectly with the outer world. It can, but need not, be activated by events in the outer world.

Thinking is followed by another function, *feeling*. When we know what a thing is, this usually evokes a certain feeling in us. That is, every perceived sensation whose meaning we are conscious of is accompanied by a certain feeling "tone." To be sure, when we isolate such a feeling tone, we are once more drawing an artificial line. Only in a few cases are we able to isolate feeling, namely, when we do not know what the perceived matter is. Feeling is first and foremost a reaction of the psyche in terms of acceptance or rejection of a perception: in other words, whether it makes a pleasurable or unpleasurable impression on us. It is an evaluation: "pleasant" or "unpleasant." We can already tell by the word if feeling accepts or rejects the matter. To like a thing or not to like it—this is feeling in its most primitive form. There are many shades and degrees of intensity of feeling, however. Language often gives occasion to misunderstandings concerning the functions. In the German language, for instance, we often confound "feeling" [*Gefühl*] and "sensation" [*Empfindung*]. Usually, such confusion does little harm because context makes evident what is meant. In French or English, however, language does already make such a distinction: French sentiment/sensation, English feeling/sensation. Even Schiller and Goethe often confound these two words, using *Empfindung* to denote a noble and sublime feeling. Psychologically speaking, "sensation" stands for a sensory perception, and "feeling" for the process of the subjective evaluation that follows every sensory perception or determination of meaning.

These three functions have already given us quite a good idea of the entire process of consciousness. One thing, however, is still missing; we have not yet established everything about this thing once we know what it *is*, what it *means*, and how we *valuate* it. We have not yet ascertained its progress in time, its whither and hither, its consonance with other things, its stylistic or musical affiliations, the context to which it belongs—things we are unable to grasp intellectually at the moment, and can only have a faint idea of. What we lack is the invisible aura that surrounds the thing.

Now if we assume that this "thing" is another person, this person will not be fully described by saying that he exists, that he is such and such a person, and perhaps even a pleasant fellow. So much past and future clings to a person, so much atmosphere, things that can be deduced only by *intuition*, a term used as much as it is misused. In German, it is best rendered as

Ahnung.⁵⁶ In effect, the latter is an excellent term while "intuition" can have many different meanings.⁵⁷ It has recently entered the language of philosophy and even everyday language: for example, in English and French. In philosophy, "intuition" already exists as a cognitive function. There is even a book by Lossky, *The Intuitive Basis of Knowledge*.⁵⁸ Bergson also describes his philosophy as an intuitive philosophy.⁵⁹ By all means, we can acknowledge that Bergson conceived the notions of *durée créatrice* and *élan vital* quite intuitively, that he *erahnte* [divined] them. It is significant, however, that he did not invent them. These ideas already existed in the Neoplatonists or the Stoics. For Proclus,⁶⁰ for instance, time has a creative meaning. Bergson did not quite realize that his theory goes back to very ancient precursors: not only to the [ideas of the] Neoplatonists, but also to ancient Persian notions in Zarathustra, such as the idea of the *Zrvan akarana*, the endless duration, in which everything comes into being.⁶¹ The notion of the creative God is a rather primitive one, in that it is a personification of an idea, so to speak. But we misunderstand this mode of thinking in primitives. We imagine a clever elderly gentleman explaining to his disciples: "Imagine this interminably long duration becomes a small man!" Or a teacher trying to make a stupid pupil understand the idea and inventing an endless snake in order to make it clearer. But, in reality, the primitive sees the image first. A strange figure appears to him, called *Zrvan akarana*, and then he tries to find out what it means. The personified picture comes first. Bergson only revived—or rather re-perceived—this primordial image through intuition. There is a similar example in the history of energetics. Robert Mayer's discovery of the philosophy of energetics⁶² was the intuition of a primordial image, as

---

⁵⁶ Presentiment, inkling, hunch.

⁵⁷ That is, in the German language.

⁵⁸ Lossky (1906). Nikolay Onufriyevich Lossky (1870–1965) was a Russian philosopher. He called his philosophy "intuitive-personalism."

⁵⁹ Bergson (1907). Henri Bergson (1859–1941) was the famous French philosopher, held in high esteem by Jung, who often quoted him in his works, with particular reference to the notions of *durée créatrice* and *élan vital*. He also noted that his own "constructive method" corresponded to Bergson's "intuitive method" (Jung, 1917, p. 399).

⁶⁰ Proclus Lycaeus (412–485), called the Successor, was a Greek Neoplatonist philosopher. In his philosophy, the monad of Time is before temporal things, and the intellect is outside of Time. He composed eighteen arguments for the eternity of the world. Cf. Lang, 2005.

⁶¹ *Zrvan akarana*, the "infinitely long duration" or "boundless time" (also: "duration in a circle") that creates Ahura Mazda and Ahriman. On *Zrvan akarana*, Chronos, Bergson's *durée creatrice*, and the notion of time in general, cf. Jung, 1911/12, § 425, and Jung, 1987, pp. 205–206.

⁶² That is, the law of energy conservation. In 1841 Julius Robert von Mayer (1814–1878), a German physician and physicist, formulated the law of the conservation of energy

in primitive philosophy there exists a model for the construct of primordial energy. The concept of energy is as a rule summed up by the term *mana*. This is a Polynesian word, which stands for "extraordinarily effective"— the force of life, health, magic, and the power of a chieftain. A great man has *mana*. When they hear a gramophone for the first time, the primitives exclaim: "*mana!*," just as we say "Jesus!" or "Oh, my God!" *Mana* also designates something that is meaningful: for instance, a meaningful or significant dream is called *manano*.

Intuition is defined as a "function of perception by unconscious means." There is no indication of either *how* intuition perceives or indeed *what* it perceives. It can perceive feelings, thoughts, and fantasies in other people. Intuitives read your character; "they can see straight into your spinal cord"; they see what's in your bag and sense, so to speak, what you have had for lunch.

Intuitive persons notice the most remarkable things. The most pronounced degree of intuition—what the Scots call "second sight"—occurs in so-called clairvoyants, who are able to divine incredibly much. This is the same divinatory capacity as that instinct in animals that allows them to anticipate earthquakes or storms. Certain people also possess this ability. A fair number of scientific discoveries have been made by intuition rather than by the thinking intellect. The intellect as such is a strangely sterile function, if it is not accompanied by the function of *Ahnung*. Intuition can perceive in a quite "illegitimate" way. We have simply no idea how those things enter into our heads. I have therefore defined intuition as that particular perceptional function that occurs via the unconscious. Nothing else beyond this definition can be said because intuition is to all intents and purposes an unreasonable dimension—as little as the logic of a woman fits into a textbook on logic. But neither will you dispute the fact that a woman has her own logic!

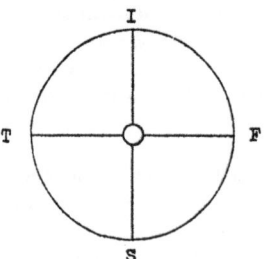

To arrange the functions in the psychic system, the horizon circle is a very simple orientation scheme. It can be divided at leisure into 360 degrees or into the four points of the compass.

The functions are situated at the four points of the compass. They can be arbitrarily moved from point to point, but not in their relation to

---

(energy can be neither created nor destroyed), one of the earliest versions of the first law of thermodynamics.

each other, which is fixed. One matter is important, however, namely that these functions are strangely interrelated. Thus it strikes us that a certain contradiction exists between the functions of thinking and feeling. There exists an unchanging opposition, even a kind of war, between them. If you feel something about an object, then you cannot think about it properly at the same time, and if you think about it, you cannot feel it properly, because either the one or the other process will be disturbed. The reason for this is that feeling implies a particular choice, excluding others. I will feel instinctively attracted to the pleasant object. I must set aside my feeling so that I can be objective, for instance, and deal objectively with quite unsavory or even downright repulsive objects. That is why a distinct feeling type presumes that the thinker is quite unfeeling. The cool objectivity of the intellect appears to the function of feeling as something like a crime against the sacred feeling.[63] Paul Bourget tells a story of a married couple waiting in the antechamber of a parliamentary office, and the wife comments on everyone who appears. At the sight of a shrewd professor, she exclaims: *Voilà un homme méchant! Il est sûrement de la police secrete!* [What a wicked man! He is surely from the secret police!][64] This is how thinking appears to the feeling type. In contrast, the thinker will look upon the feeling person as an outright imbecile. As a matter of fact, these two groups of persons do not get along well at all.

The worst case, however, is the misunderstanding within the soul of the individual person when, for instance, a distinct feeling type crushes his own thinking against a wall. It takes a very long time to reach the point where the two functions are workably united. A thinking type will

---

[63] On the opposition between thinking and feeling see, apart from the discussion in *Psychological Types* (1921), the live enactment, so to speak, of this contrast in the letters between the alleged "thinking type" Jung and the "feeling type" Hans Schmid-Guisan (Jung & Schmid-Guisan, 2013).

[64] Jung also quotes this passage from a novel, *L'Étape* (1902), by Paul Bourget (1852–1935), a French novelist and critic, in 1943, § 233, and, at length, in the *Visions Seminar* (1997, p. 805): "A little bourgeois couple were waiting in the antechamber of the office of the Minister of Public Education, watching the people who came and went, and tremendously impressed with the solemnity and grandeur of the place. The woman was very much thrilled and thought that each person who entered was probably a diplomat, perhaps an ambassador, because only very great people would be in that place! But the Minister had asked a philosopher to come in, who was a bit of a recluse and lived a very quiet life in the country; he wanted to consult him about a certain matter. And that man had the features of a man who thinks, and was somewhat forlorn in appearance, so when he walked into the room and had to wait too, the little woman stared at him and said: 'Il est de la police secrète, il a l'air si méchant!'"

establish all kinds of theories, for example, only to deny his all too soft heart. But sometimes it does re-emerge all the same—and how!

The same observation can be made about sensation and intuition. To what extent are sensory perception and perception by intuition contradictory? The contradiction as such is not inherent. One should be able to assume that we can look at things—and let them take effect on us as they are—and entertain all kinds of intuitions about them just the same. Strangely enough, this is not so. If you intend to engage in exact observation—looking through a microscope, for instance—you must exclude all the possibilities swirling around you, just as we close our eyes when thinking in order to concentrate and not to be distracted by sensory impressions. Pure observation—whether with your ears, your sense of touch, or your eyes—must necessarily eliminate, as far as possible, anything else that could also be present.

One can even tell by observing people that whoever sees things does not look at them. The eyes of the watcher or observer always have a certain sharply delineated character given the intersection of the visual axes. In the intuitive person, by contrast, we observe the strange phenomenon that he does not look at things, but sees. His eyes "illuminate" things, usually with wide eyes. Take for instance Stieler's portrait of Goethe:[65] the eyes radiate; this is the gaze of the intuitive person. Highly intuitive persons often have a somewhat veiled look, so that you cannot even tell whom or what they are looking at; it is as if they were looking through things. Those people do not even look at you or your everyday face, but at something imponderable, atmospheric, at something perhaps that you might not want to know or believe.

Just as the sensation or perception of objects does not allow for intuition at the same time, intuition excludes exact sensation or perception of the object. Pure intuitives possess a truly remarkable capacity for non-observation. For instance, they can spend months in a room without being able to tell its color, how it is furnished, etc. They will make certain statements about it without, however, being able to verify them through observation. They will be able to intuit what is inside the drawers but will have no idea what the chest of drawers or cupboard looks like.

So we have a system of four functions that intersect one another. There are two pairs of opposites that differ in one other respect: thinking as well

---

[65] Joseph Karl Stieler (1781–1858), a German painter, best known for his neoclassical portraits. There are numerous reproductions of his portrait of Goethe (1828) on the Internet.

as feeling both claim to be reasonable functions, thinking in particular, but also feeling, because you must have reasonable, aesthetic, or ethical values to be adjusted. If sensation or intuition wants to be reasonable, however, this will be a great mistake. If you adopt a "reasonable" attitude when observing, you will not see the unexpected. The same is true for intuition; you cannot intuit with some sophisticated intention in mind. The very essence of these two functions is to perceive what is there, however unexpected it may be. If, for instance, a clairvoyant turns professional and then applies his art in a rational way, he will easily slip up and have to resort to all kinds of tricks to replace his failing intuition. In fact, what these people see is generally the last thing people expect or want to hear, so that it is very hard for clairvoyants to remain honest toward their gifts. So thinking and feeling are rational functions; and sensation and intuition are irrational functions, which can only be fully exercised if they are not subject to rational restrictions.

Each of these functions possesses a specific energy inherent to it, a certain measure of psychic energy. If one function is suppressed, a loss of energy will occur. The energy is displaced into the unconscious, causing certain disorders. To a certain extent, these functions can be used at will: that is to say, we can apply them—intensify or diminish them. In principle, this is true for all the functions, with one restriction, however. No one can use all four in equal measure. When—as is usually the case—one of the functions is particularly well developed in someone, this function can be increased to an exceptionally great degree, which can also happen when it is deliberately applied to certain objects. At least one of the other functions is not developed, however, often two, and sometimes even three. Every highly developed function is opposed by an underdeveloped one. This is not a value judgment. I simply mean that the latter function is inferior, not adjusted and undifferentiated in *comparison* to the developed function. Someone with particularly well-developed sensation, for instance, will find his intuition in an unconscious, deplorable state, that is to say, in an archaic and undeveloped condition.

The exclusive thinker is inferior in his feeling. Now every thinker will immediately tell you what marvelous feelings he has—which actually proves us right—for he thus reveals that he does not control them and consequently must suppress them as an uncomfortable disturbance. Vice versa, someone with the most finely differentiated feeling can exhibit a kind of archaic thinking that is truly astounding. Usually, this is so embarrassing that these matters are covered up. It is well known that many great thinkers dread women very much, because women affect their feelings. The thinker avoids situations that stir up his feelings, and so he ends up marrying his housekeeper!

If these functions are not applied consciously, they will work automatically. "It thinks" in you, without your wanting it to, or "it feels" in you. The third possibility is that the process occurs entirely in the unconscious. "It thinks in you without your noticing it." Or the feeling process takes place in you quite mindless of the fact that you are unaware of feeling anything—it is proceeding in the unconscious nevertheless. Unconscious feeling processes can be evidenced by experiments, for instance, without the person concerned having the slightest inkling of them.

In addition to these functions, we must also mention other things in consciousness. For the functions are not suspended in empty space, but are related to a center, to the "I." They may appear as activities of the I, or, on the contrary, the I may appear as their object, as their victim. For only what is related to this I is conscious. The I is a complex of all kinds of psychic and organic facts; it is given by the physical reality of the body and by the general feelings related to the body. People thus point to their bodies and say: "That's me." But psychic processes, too, are an undeniable reality. When you say: "I think, therefore I am," you perceive the psychic process of thinking: *cogito, ergo sum*.[66] But it would also be perfectly possible to say: "I feel, therefore I am." Or: "I am thought, therefore I am." Or: "I am felt."

There also exist intermediate levels between these functions. Natural scientists are most often empirical thinkers: that is, their predominant functions are thinking and sensation. Thinkers like Schopenhauer, on the other hand, are speculative thinkers: that is, his predominant function lies between thinking and intuition.

---

[66] A dictum famously introduced by René Descartes (1596–1650) in his *Discours de la méthode* (1637, part 4, chapter 3). Cf. Jung's discussion of Descartes in the previous semester (2018, pp. 2–3 and note 61).

Lecture 4

18 MAY 1934

LAST TIME WE talked about the functions of consciousness. In the literature, you will find a detailed description of these functions in my book *Psychological Types* (1921), and in the chapter on "Definitions" a philosophical and psychological debate on the concept of functions. It does of course make for somewhat difficult reading. I gave a briefer description in an essay in my book *Seelenprobleme der Gegenwart* [Psychic problems of our time].[67] Gerhard Adler provides a very good description of the functions in the context of so-called typology in his new book *Die Entdeckung der Seele* [The discovery of the soul].[68] Other discussions of the subject are more or less non-existent in German, except for a few articles in the professional literature, and the short description by Kranefeldt in the Göschen booklet.[69] Unfortunately, a few mistakes found their way into the book, but it is none the less worthwhile. Publications in English include a translation from Dutch, *Character and the Unconscious*.[70] A very interesting book, also in English, was written by my former collaborator

---

[67] "A psychological theory of types" (1928 [1931]); in Jung, 1931.

[68] Adler (1934); with a foreword by Jung. Gerhard Adler (1904–1988) was an analytical psychologist of German-Jewish extraction; he lived in Berlin until 1936, then in London. He was editor of Jung's selected letters, co-editor of the *Collected Works* in English, and two-term president of the IAAP (1971–1977). Cf. Jung, 1952 [1949]; 1972, pp. 127, 213–214; 1973, pp. 184–185; Kirsch, 2000; Shamdasani, 2005, pp. 48–51.

[69] Kranefeldt, 1930. Wolfgang M. Kranefeldt (1892–1950) was a German physician and psychotherapist. During the Nazi era, he was a member of the governing body of the Goering Institute (Kirsch, 2000, p. 133). The *Sammlung Göschen*, a series of low-cost books, provided "clear, easily understandable, and concise introductions to all areas of science and technology," with the final goal of giving "a consistent and systematic representation of our complete knowledge" (from the series introduction).

[70] Van der Hoop, 1923. Johannes Hermanus van der Hoop (1887–1950) was a Dutch psychiatrist. He underwent analysis with both C. G. Jung and Freudian Ruth Mack Brunswick. He was a co-founder and president of the Dutch Association for Psychotherapy and a lecturer at the University of Amsterdam.

Dr. Hinkle, *The Recreating of the Individual,* which also includes a discussion of the theory of functions.[71]

Today, let us discuss some further aspects of these functions. They can be used arbitrarily: that is, they are subject to the will and can be directed, so that for example one can think in a consciously directed manner. In the case of feeling, however, this is not so obvious to us. This accounts for the small difference between the male and the female type of loving. Men do not understand that this can be done, because none of them can do it, as it were. If you are married or have otherwise experienced altercations in matters of the heart, you will know that differences of opinion do exist. "If you only wanted, you could direct your feeling," we might hear. And in fact one can to some extent direct one's feelings, just as one can direct one's thoughts and perceptions. Some persons are highly skilled in this respect. Others are able to think hypothetically; they can think abstractly on purpose: for instance, they can make an absurd assumption and draw conclusions from it—a real miracle for people who cannot think in a direct and willful manner.

The same is true for feeling. It simply depends on which of your functions is domesticated. Usually it is the women who can direct their feeling, and men who can control their thinking. Now if such men pass judgment on feelings, they will therefore reach the conclusion that a feeling is something one simply has, but that one cannot alter one's feelings deliberately in any way. This is not true, however. It is amazing what people with differentiated feeling can accomplish with it, especially when they want something! Let us suppose, for instance, that a feeling type accompanies someone to a party. He—or more likely she—would rather not go, and will groan over it in thought or in speech. Then when they arrive, however, she thinks, *Why, there is a nice feeling here after all, a nice atmosphere, it will be all right.* So they stay at the party, everything goes smoothly, and everybody says, "What a nice evening!" The feeling type goes home, however, and thinks: "Yes, but I paid for it." And this is quite true. Or a woman can change her husband's mood for the better when he returns home in the evening by deliberately showing him some feelings.

---

[71] Hinkle, 1923. Beatrice Moses Hinkle (1874–1953) was a pioneering American physician. In 1905, she was appointed as San Francisco's city physician, thus becoming the first woman physician in the United States to hold a public position. Moving to New York in 1908, she founded, with Charles R. Dana, the country's first therapeutic clinic, at Cornell Medical School. After studying with Freud and Jung in Europe, she played an important role in the Jungian community in New York and in disseminating Jung's ideas through her translations, e.g., *Psychology of the Unconscious* (Jung, 1911/12).

One can also intuit deliberately, that is, in a directed manner. There are people who often say, "Oh, but I knew it!" But only after the fact—we are not aware of the premonition at the moment we have it. Of all the functions, intuition seems the most unpredictable and unmanageable, and most people only know of intuition as the vaguest hunches coming from heaven knows where. There are also people, however, who literally live by this function and behold everything intuitively, as if they were drawing out the soul from things. In doing so, something does in fact keep occurring to them, and then they take this seriously. They even treat it as a fact, as if the other had indeed said or done this.

All these functions can also occur involuntarily in consciousness. Thus we can think, feel, sense, and intuit involuntarily. These involuntary processes can also proceed unconsciously, however, and this is when matters become interesting. You can perceive unconsciously, and even think unconsciously. The question is merely, how do you determine this? This must be deduced indirectly, that is, through inference from subsequent action. One finds out that at some stage a thought process must have intervened in the unconscious. Also in dreams: There you can often find very complicated, even philosophical thought processes, often of considerable depth.

Likewise one can feel unconsciously. In effect, this occurs quite often, especially in love relationships, when we have unconscious feelings we ourselves are not aware of, but which are nonetheless registered by our environment—particularly by intuitive types—in our facial expressions, which are usually beyond our control. You can also infer such unconscious feeling from subsequent actions, and also from dreams. As a quite common rule, certain feeling states, which had not been realized because they were unpleasant or inopportune, reappear at night in dreams. For instance, you have made someone's acquaintance during the day, had the impression that this man is a pleasant gentleman, and that all is well. That night, however, you have an unpleasant dream, with a dreadful affect against this man. You have received an unconscious, negative impression of something you did not want to see, because it would have interfered with your image or spoilt the pleasant evening. This is like a dark stain. We don't like dark stains, however. When we like something, we would like it to be perfect. This dark stain then produces unpleasant feeling associations, which can reappear to us in a dream or in other after-effects. If perceptions should actually have produced an affect in you, the respective affect impressions can appear to you unconsciously in a dream. Physical affect symptoms are also possible, or states of anxiety, etc.

Unconscious perceptions or impressions can often express themselves in very strange ways. One case in point is that of an Englishman, a big game hunter, who was hunting tigers in India and came near a watering hole toward sunset. He climbed a tree and waited for night to fall. When the sun set, a wind picked up, as is common in such regions. The first gust seized him with a tremendous fear. He was afraid to climb down the tree, however—because otherwise he might have been perceived as prey—and controlled himself. The next gust heightened his sense of panic. When the third gust came, he could no longer bear the situation. He thought it was God warning him and climbed down. At this moment, the tree collapsed. It had been hollowed out by termites.[72] All hunters living in such regions know this, and will obviously realize it when climbing up such a tree. In the excitement of the tiger hunt, however, the Englishman had not wanted to notice this, because it was the only possible tree in the area. So it would have been very unpleasant for him to realize that the tree was hollowed out by termites. Obviously, he would have had to see this, because he had climbed the tree in daylight, but he overlooked it. The unconscious noticed it, however, and warned him when the wind picked up: "Aha, here it comes!" These are unconscious sensations.

Naturally, there are also unconscious intuitions. Since intuitions are never completely conscious, intuition is a strange borderline function. Perhaps you know H. G. Wells's fantastic tale, *The Time Machine*.[73] The book's protagonist invented an engine that functions not in space, but in time. If one sits in the machine, one travels—not forward or backward in space but in time. This apparatus stands on four quartz pillars. Three are plainly visible while the fourth, which is always blurred, is never clearly visible, since it represents the time function. Intuition is like this. It is a function that is never really tangible, and we know as much of it as we do of the fourth dimension. Therefore, my definition of intuition is somewhat makeshift, and in fact a declaration of scientific bankruptcy: "Intuition is perception via the unconscious."

Sometimes intuitions and sensations are triggered by something like the termite holes.[74] For example, a patient consulted me. I received her in my garden house, where a breeze came through the door. "Oh," she said, "a gentleman has been to see you!" I was really amazed that she knew this,

---

[72] As Jung also noted elsewhere, termites "hollow out trees . . . so that they remain standing as if in perfect condition. Then comes a storm, and everything collapses. So when you pitch camp under a tree, you must always check to see if there aren't any termite tracks, otherwise the tree could land on your head" (Jung, 2014, p. 95).

[73] Wells, 1895. H.[erbert] G.[eorge] Wells (1866–1946), the well-known English author, knew Jung, met him on several occasions, and credited him for the inspiration he got from Jung's ideas and writings.

[74] This phrase only in Hannah (p. 103).

as I had seen him before lunch, and she could not have met him. "You know, I'm very intuitive, and I simply notice things like this." Suddenly I looked at my ashtray—and saw cigarette butts. I never smoke cigarettes myself. So this was obviously the patient's unconscious perception. In actual fact, however, we simply have no knowledge *how* people come to have these perceptions.

The curious occurrence of serial events, that is, that things tend to occur in numbers, also belongs into this area: "What divides in twain, divides in threes," and "It never rains but it pours." It often happens that people make cocksure predictions. Thus a professor told his students: "This is truly a rare case, and the next is sure to follow straightaway." This was an elderly professor in Würzburg, a very strange fellow, as psychiatrists often are.[75] The entire primitive and Eastern science rests upon the principle of the random series. This is important to note because everything that the East has developed to such a degree is lacking in our conscious mind, is completely underdeveloped with us, and lies in the unconscious. Only sometimes do we hit upon it. So that is why such serial events are important, which appear so strange when they do happen.

They often occur in a banal form. Only the other day, twenty-four hours ago, I took down *Ulysses* by James Joyce to show to an Englishman, something I rarely do, and certainly have not done during the past three or four years.[76] "How come you are doing this?" he said. "I was in a bookshop just a few days ago, saw this book, and thought, *That's a book I ought to have*—even though I had never heard of it!"

For us, such events seem to be absolute coincidences; for other kinds of people, however, these events constitute an actual regularity, and they consider our causality to be superstition and something ludicrous. The East already discovered the laws of coincidence long ago. The same applies to the primitives, for whom there is no doubt that if one unfavorable thing should occur, several others will immediately come to pass. Thus they know favorable and unfavorable days. The so-called superstition of mariners, hunters in alpine regions, and so forth, is also not actual superstition but quite ordinary cleverness: that is, the science of people who live

---

[75] "The law of the duplication of cases is known to all doctors engaged in clinical work. An old professor of psychiatry at Würzburg always used to say of a particularly rare clinical case: 'Gentlemen, this case is absolutely unique—tomorrow we shall have another just like it.' I myself often observed the same thing during my eight years' practice in an insane asylum" (Jung, 1931 [1930], § 121).

[76] On Jung's attitude toward Joyce and his magnum opus (1922), see Jung, 1932—an article that aroused much criticism in the press and public. Jung also treated Joyce's daughter Lucia in 1934.

under primitive circumstances. If you find yourself among savages as the only European, you know that the first unfavorable coincidence will make people anxious and nervous, so that they will most certainly let you down the next time. Add to this the law of the series. That is why an explorer said: "Magic is the science of the jungle."[77]

This unconscious course of our function of consciousness is effectively a very comforting fact. For it allows us to expect with some certainty that what we do not think, perceive, and intuit with our consciousness will be done for us by the unconscious. This is somewhat hazardous in some respects, however, because the unconscious functions somewhat differently from consciousness. Our unconscious ways of thinking and feeling processes are characteristically altered in terms of so-called archaism, a functionality characteristic of antiquity and popular belief. The unconscious is more primitive, and therefore its conclusions do not tally with our own deductions; it works rather with analogies.

Nobody has developed all functions equally. Ordinarily, people content themselves with developing and differentiating only one function well. Someone who perceives well will content himself with a good observation of facts. He might not be able to understand them, but he will realize "how the wind blows." Or someone with a good brain will probably become a thinking type, and so forth. A thinking person might observe quite poorly, perhaps imprecisely or superficially, but he will carefully deliberate on his scant perceptions. He will think of corresponding situations, and thus adjust to reality. It is thus always the case that a part of the functions is unconscious.

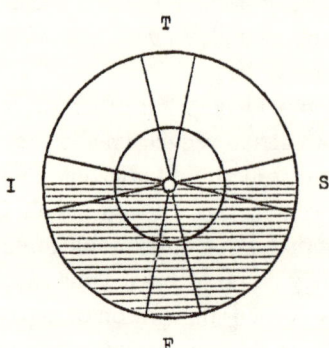

The figure depicts the thinking type. Thinking is excellent and in the top position. It is confident and deliberate in all its decisions, and it copes very well

---

[77] "Magic saves. Then it is white. Magic kills. Then it is black. It is the science of the jungle" (Vandercook, 1925, p. 194). Also quoted by Jung in "Archaic man" (1931 [1930], §§ 121, 128), and in (the revised version of) *Symbols of Transformation* (1911/12, § 221): "'Magic is the science of the jungle,' a famous explorer once said. Civilized man contemptuously looks down on primitive superstitions, which is about as sensible as turning up one's nose at the pikes and halberds, the fortresses and tall-spired cathedrals of the Middle Ages. Primitive methods are just as effective under primitive conditions as machine-guns or the radio are under modern conditions."

with all situations that require thinking. Feeling is completely in the fog, however, and has the quality of a prehistoric man, of a primitive cave man. If you observe such a person in a pronounced "feeling" situation, he will present an entirely different picture. Place this thinking type in a love situation, with which he can no longer deal by thinking or gain the upper hand with thought, and emotional storms will come to the surface, storms of a partly infantile, partly barbaric-primitive character, as with a primitive man. I have seen people whom I considered decidedly superior, and who behaved downright impossibly, ridiculously, Negro-like in an overtly emotional situation. It is as if such people could remain either only completely buttoned up in such situations, full of "self control,"[78] the perfect, cultured gentleman—or behave completely like Negroes. Add to this the lamentable fact that thinking is completely distorted by feeling in these situations. Superior thinking will then be taken hostage by the primitive affects, and the thoughts themselves become more than ridiculous. These persons are like hysterical women, and the result is a complete alteration of their personality.

Here, the thinking function is the domesticated form; the opposite feeling function is the "inferior" function, while the other two functions, intuition and sensation, are subsidiary or auxiliary functions. Often, the horizontal axis is slightly rotated so that two functions are in the light, and two are on the shadow side, but it never happens that two opposing functions are in the light at the same time. At least one function always lies in the primitive, undifferentiated darkness, and the inferior function is never in the light. Thus, although every thinking person is a feeling person in their unconscious, this feeling is archaic and explosive. In other words, you can infer the character of the unconscious from the differentiated function and its properties.

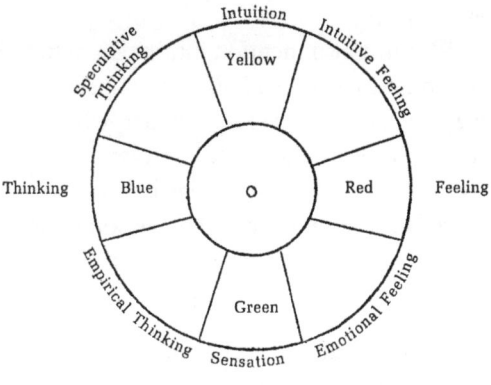

I did not discover these functions by myself. I only stumbled on this treasure trove, for the functions are an ancient fact. They are actually

---

[78] This expression in English in the notes.

age-old knowledge, which has long existed in the East, particularly in India and China. I was not aware of this, and only found the parallels to my own discoveries later on. There these functions are designated by colors, which indicate a valuation and different "feeling tones." Thus the different functions are allocated to colors with lesser or greater correspondence, just like sounds for that matter; for instance, the sound of a trumpet is a glaring blue or white, and so forth. Certain people experience certain consonances of sense, so-called synesthesias.[79]

The vast majority of people describe thinking as blue, because it has the properties of air. A thought is an air-like entity. A thought, or a prayer to God, is depicted as a bird or feather by the primitives. The Indians let down feathers fly across a precipice. God is imagined as an ascending airstream, which rises along the rock face and transports the feather into the blue sky. Thus, birds are messengers from the realm of thoughts, and the soul is depicted as a bird in old monuments. Feeling is very often represented by red, because of its associations with the heart and with blood. Intuition—but here uncertainty begins—is often given in white, or in yellow or gold, the color of the sun. Sensation, the perception of concrete objects, is often given in green, like the green surface of the Earth.

Similar color qualities are also indicated in Chinese culture, the so-called Lamaistic circle. Lamaism is a Tibetan religion, but it radiates from China to Japan. In Lamaism, this theory of functions is developed to a significant extent. There, it is called "mandala." Mandala is Sanskrit for circle. It is considered a meritorious task to paint such "magic circles" every day.[80]

We must also mention intermediate functions. These are zones in which two functions intermingle, as in speculative thinking for instance, which was the case with Schopenhauer, who was primarily a thinker, while intuition took second place. Nietzsche, by contrast, was primarily an intuitive type, and only secondarily a thinker. On the other side of intuition there is intuitive feeling. This is something invisible, but occurs very frequently, most apparent in women who know something "through their

---

[79] A phenomenon Jung had come across in his association studies (Jung & Riklin, 1904/05, §§ 139, 141) and that was also researched by his teacher Eugen Bleuler (1912) and Jung's analysand Oskar Pfister (1912).

[80] As Jung did from August to September 1917, when he was stationed in Château d'Oex near Lausanne. "While I was there I sketched every morning in a notebook a small circular drawing, a mandala, which seemed to correspond to my inner situation at the time. . . . My mandalas were cryptograms concerning the state of the self. . . . I guarded them like precious pearls" (1962, pp. 220–221).

heart." On account of this frequent blending, the terms "feeling" and "intuition" are often mixed alternatively. Then there is the intermediate stage between thinking and sensation, that is, empirical thinking, which is characteristic of natural scientists. And finally, we have the blend between feeling and sensation. Those people always try to enforce their feelings in the objective world. It is these types who are unable to refrain from informing you about their emotional state in an importunate manner, and are therefore so often the great bores at parties.

Lecture 5

25 May 1934

My last lecture prompted many questions, and I have received a number of letters. One question was whether the mixed feeling-sensation type is always such a terrible bore at social occasions. I have given a few hints about those psychological types that result from the differentiation of different functions. A whole book could be written about the topic. Naturally, such an abbreviated discussion cannot do adequate justice to the subject. Every type has a positive and a negative aspect. After all, these feeling-sensation types do not spend their entire lives in boring company, although they are inclined to have this effect in social situations. So, in order to make amends for offending the dignity of this type, let me mention that many artists, poets, and especially musicians, can be found among it.

Other questions have been raised, mostly concerning the concept of intuition.[81] This is not surprising, because this concept is extremely difficult to grasp; indeed, intangibility is its very essence. Logical terms are quite easy to delineate and to grasp, whereas empirical ones intersect—think of that column of the machine that is never clearly visible.[82] This indistinct quality is also the result of the fact that intuition is defined as a function that perceives via the unconscious. Although it can, on occasion, *clothe* itself in all of the other functions, as we saw last time in the examples of the hunter in the tree and the cigarette butts, even so it cannot be identified with such a sensory function. It can affect thinking functions, for instance, when I think about something unconsciously, and then the result of this thinking process suddenly enters consciousness. But even with all

---

[81] Particularly a long letter by one Walter Strauß of 18 May (ETH Archives), which claimed that Jung's examples of intuition (e.g., the patient in the garden house or the tiger hunter) were actually not "real" intuitions. If intuition with regard to objective events really existed, Strauß argued, this would be the end of roulette, because such an intuitive would break any casino bank.

[82] In H. G. Wells's *Time Machine*; see the previous lecture.

the will in the world and the most thorough investigation you will not be able to prove how someone arrives at this knowledge. This includes a considerable number of cases that stand at the limits of our knowledge—and intuition lives on this border. Ladies and gentlemen! We know far from everything! Compared to what one could know, our knowledge is very limited indeed.

For the sake of clarity, let me briefly define intuition:[83]

I. Intuition is a basic psychological function. It is the particular function that conveys perceptions in an unconscious manner.
II. Everything can be the object of this perception, both outer and inner objects, or connections between them.
III. It is important to note that intuition is neither a function of sensation nor of feeling or thinking.
IV. Like sensation, intuition is an irrational perceptional function.
V. As in the case of sensation, the contents of intuition have the character of a given, of a given fact, quite in contrast to the thinking or feeling functions, whose contents have the character of something derived or deduced.[84]
VI. Intuition is not an intra-psychic function, but can cover everything: death, life, health, illness, the weather, the stock exchange, anything that exists in nature.
VII. You will find intuitive types among hunters, stock exchange speculators—the fortunate ones, that is—and in all possible professions in which a systematic, routine kind of work is less needed, but rather ingenious apprehension. The intuitive type abounds among artists, doctors, and judges of character in general.

One of the questions concerns my remarks on the law of the series.[85] If any regularity existed in this respect that could be spotted by intuition, the casino banks would surely have been broken at some point. This is a

---

[83] The following description closely follows the one Jung had given in the "Definitions" chapter of *Psychological Types* (1921).

[84] Hannah adds: "Spinoza thought it the highest type of knowledge that exists" (p. 106). Cf. Jung, 1921, § 770: "Intuitive knowledge possesses an intrinsic certainty and conviction, which enabled Spinoza (and Bergson) to uphold the *scientia intuitiva* as the highest form of knowledge." Baruch (Benedict) de Spinoza (1632–1677), the great philosopher, distinguished in his *Ethics* (1677; part II, proposition 40, note 2) between three kinds of knowledge: the first kind is opinion, or imagination; the second, reason and knowledge; and the third, and highest, intuition.

[85] See the previous lecture and note 49.

very clever point. While serial cases do exist, every given situation is like a prison for the intuitive type, which is quite a contrast to the sensation type. Intuitives feverishly search for new possibilities, but can use their function only to a very limited extent in a particular situation. I actually once had a patient who used to travel to Monte Carlo whenever she was broke. I told her: "Listen, this is a very dangerous thing to do!" But she replied: "Not for me!" Later I saw her there and asked her: "How is business?" She said: "The right moment hasn't yet come. I go to the casino every day. Unfortunately, I cannot break the bank. I can only work out one series in advance at a time." Then she staked and won. Intuition is like that; it can only be used to gain a certain modest advantage. If an intuitive is really down to his last penny, intuition appears to have an interest in giving him just enough to go on with, but no more. If you are a clairvoyant, for instance, this will not be enough to make a fortune. You cannot move mountains with sheer instinct, but it will help you pan just the amount of gold you need to survive. If you want more, you will have to make use of a second function. We have four functions, after all, so as to be able to meet all situations. Intuition does not always work; nor does thinking. There are certain things you cannot think about. So we also have feeling and the other functions to be able to adjust to situations that cannot be thought about. If you take a brilliant thinker like Kant, who can develop a thought and hold it for a period of time that is as long as the *Critique of Pure Reason*, and you cast him into a personal situation, he will not be able to think.

* * *

Today, let us conclude the discussion of the theory of functions, and then consider some other facts. There is one peculiar function that is set above the others and is characteristic of consciousness: that is the function of the volitional faculty [*Willensvermögen*], in short, the *will*. If it were on a par with the other functions, we might call it a fifth function, but it is better to see it as a superordinate, central function of the I. It reflects the fact that a certain amount of energy is freely available in consciousness, like a mobile division or reserve unit. This psychically available energy stands at the disposal of consciousness. So one can, for instance, engage in concentrated thinking and feeling. With the will, one can direct, intensify, diminish, or suppress the functions. It is thus a dynamic function of the I. Evidently, this function is subject to certain conditions. It cannot will under all circumstances. Sometimes the will is interrupted by other situations, by impulsive breakthroughs, drives, which emerge from the I. So long as the I is not exhausted, however, it enjoys total freedom in its use of this mobile power reserve. But the will is indeed exhaustible. When you are tired, your will wanes, and a sort of demoralized state ensues.

The will is not an instinct, however, but an achievement of our cultural history. We have gradually created a reserve of will, which has been wrested from nature. The will is a distinct cultural phenomenon. When the will is depicted in an image or dreamt of, it is always represented as an instrument, as a weapon, an apparatus, a knife, or something similar. This means that it is something humans made.

Primitives have no such will, for will is not a drive. What looks like will in primitives is in fact their drive; in other words, they do not "will" what they want. There is a tribe of cave dwellers, whom I recently visited.[86] Their language is still reminiscent of the sounds of nature; the cock, for instance, is *quikondi*, the hen: *ga ga*, and the lament so frequently heard in these parts: *kungum kungum*. At some point, I had to choose my messenger among the members of this tribe, a good 120 kilometers away from the Uganda railway, which was being built at the time. A man, a very good runner, was brought before me. I gave him the letters, and told him: "Now take these to the white man who lives in the great beast—that is, the steam locomotive—for the whites live in houses on wheels." Thus I gave him the letters, but he just stared at me open-mouthed and remained standing, just as stupidly even after the interpreter had spoken to him. Then came our "headman,"[87] who was just as black as the runner: "You know, these are really stupid Negroes. You can't talk to him that way. I'll show you how to do it!" He took a whip, brandished it, cursed the messenger, his children and his children's children, his ancestors, and so forth, and in the end lashed his behind. He got him into a great state of excitement about the letters of the white chief waiting here, and about the other white chief waiting for them in his great beast, and he drew a picture of the runner as an arrow in between them. Finally, the messenger started to move his feet, dashed off and, would you believe it, never stopped running until he had covered the entire 120 kilometers. It was just a matter of putting him in the right mood.

Among[88] the Australian natives, if a man is murdered by someone in the next tribe, it is of no use whatsoever to hold a council to discuss this, for

---

[86] Jung is referring here to his expedition to the Elgonyis in 1925 (Jung, 1962, pp. 282 ff.).
[87] This expression in English in the notes.
[88] This paragraph is taken (with slight stylistic adjustments) from Hannah (p. 107). It is only fragmentary in Sidler, and missing in Schärf.

they are not in the least interested. They have to be worked up into a state of rage. A rite is performed on the man in question, a kind of coital movement, until he is really angry. Then he is pulled by the beard, and the man jumps up: "They killed my brother!" Then they dash off, and if they meet a man from the other tribe, they will kill him and the matter is settled. If they don't find anybody, however, their rage wears off, they go home and everything has to be started all over again. You see, such a tribe is just a lazy mass, with no energy at its disposal, unless they are put into the mood by a *rite d'entrée*. Will is a human accomplishment, and therefore always the sign of a higher culture.

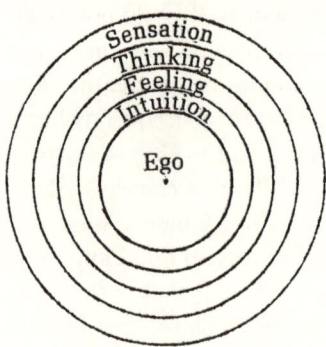

Now let me turn to another group of psychic functions, even though the term "function" is somewhat doubtful here; it would be more appropriate to speak of basic psychic conditions. Here is a diagram.

Consciousness can be depicted as a limited area, in which sensation is the strongest function in this case. Depending on type, of course, any other function could be the superior one. Now all these sensory perceptions are not conscious at all, unless they are related to an "I." The I is the center to which everything refers. Although it

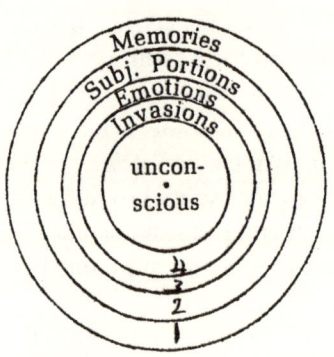

is what is nearest to us, it is in actual fact something quite unknown, something highly mysterious, a great conundrum. Nothing is conscious that is not related to an I. We can only describe it from the outside. The I, for instance, is the sensation of my entire body and of my environment, my thoughts and feelings and intuitions, and beyond this something else.

If I have a sensation or a thought, their content is not just a given fact, but something is added to it that comes from our inside. When I see a painting, for instance, it "reminds me of something." Besides that memory, or subordinated to it, there appears the so-called subjective part of the consciousness function. In the case of thinking, this means that I cannot conceive a single thought without some content appearing automatically in me, which then assimilates itself with this outside. It is this content that enables me to have a thought in the first place. That is, I cannot have a single thought without first having an inner notion of it. For the mind is neither a *tabula rasa* nor a blank slate. We make the great mistake of thinking that children are born as a *tabula rasa*, but this is not the case.[89] There exists an unconscious, in which all representations of ideas are already given in the genetic material, so to speak. Everything is already laid down in the inherited memory of mankind. This is where the subjective part of all psychic functions comes from.

If you have a sensation or a perception, a fact pushes forward from inside, which might or might not be processed in the end. In any event, you will always keep back something. If someone asks you, "What are you thinking?," you will single out something and exclude everything else. You will have a main thought and beside it a large number of secondary thoughts, which you wisely keep to yourself. And this is how it must be, for otherwise there would be no individuality. Otherwise, we could simply all be identical, and we would be like termites. These secondary thoughts make the I the keeper of the great seal of all secrets. Here we are already approaching the neighborhood of the unconscious, in which all those matters are kept that are better not thought of—the so-called repressions.

On the one hand, the inner field of the I, which we can imagine as a hollow sphere, is something plastic in which experiences have imprinted themselves, that is, molds of memory or so-called engrams[90] that have impressed themselves in the plastic mass of the psyche. On the other hand, this "inside" is not only a plastic surface. It also has a life of its own. It can even produce very powerful things, namely affects and emotions. The term "affect" means a condition that has been brought about; the Latin *affectum* indicates that which has been done to me. "Emotion," on the other hand, refers to something that breaks out or erupts; *emotio* = an outward movement. In a state of affect, I am affected: "He did it to me!"

Thus, there is a third layer, that of emotions. It is frequently confused with feeling, but it is something different. Feeling always involves evaluation, it is a valuing function, whereas emotion is involuntary; in affect

---

[89] This phrase appears only in Hannah (p. 108). This view was stressed many times by Jung in his works.

[90] A term coined by the German zoologist, evolutionary biologist, and memory researcher Richard Semon (1859–1918), for memory traces or after-effects of stimulation that conserve the changes in the nervous system (Semon, 1921).

you are always a victim.[91] If I am a great artist, I will be able to depict a feeling artificially, but this is never genuine. Genuine affect exists whenever I am overwhelmed by an emotional state. You are not at all human in a state of affect, but a senseless mass. Affects are kinds of explosions that come from the inside. Consequently, emotions have nothing to do with feeling; they are psycho-physical states.

The James-Lange theory of affects states that affect is only a matter of feeling certain visceral or vasomotor changes.[92] For instance, you find a situation troublesome or annoying. Well, that is a feeling. When matters go too far, however, and your vascular system becomes innervated, your blood vessels will become dilated. You will "go red in the face," and thereafter you will "lose your head." You will start to suppress your breathing, and so forth.

A fourth group or layer is about something that transcends emotions. Emotions are in actual fact conditions mainly characterized by their physiological effects. They are affective states that are hard to define in precise terms. In this layer, however, we find the so-called invasions from the unconscious. Their contents are tangible and can be put into words.

---

[91] This phrase only in Hannah (p. 109).

[92] This theory was developed independently by William James (1842–1910), the famous Harvard psychologist and philosopher, and the Danish physiologist Carl Lange (1834–1900). Strictly speaking, it refers to the origin and nature of emotions, not affects, and states that all emotion is derived from the presence of a stimulus, which evokes a physiological response, which in turn makes a person feel a specific emotion. The theory has been variously criticized, but it has also been argued that at least a part of it is still valid. Jung held James in high esteem. They first met at Clark University in 1909. Jung called him "one of the most outstanding persons that he had ever met" and "a model" (in Shamdasani, 2003, p. 58).

Lecture 6

1 June 1934

ONE CORRESPONDENT HAS written to inquire exactly what individuality is.[93] I am unable to answer this question in this context, even more so as this question is not germane to our present subject matter. What we are dealing with here is the "I." There is a considerable difference between the "I" and "individuality": The I is the consciousness of one's "suchness" [*So-sein*], whereas individuality *is* that suchness. Individuality, that is, the self, extends far beyond the I. The self is an empirical matter, not one that exists *a priori*. The fact that we are conscious of our I does not mean that we know anything about our character and so on; for that matter, it is only in the course of life, indeed in the evening of life, that we can say who we really are.

* * *

Let us continue with our actual subject matter, and first recapitulate the diagram.

The outermost surface of our spheric consciousness is characterized, in this example, by sensation. Intuition thus lies innermost; in this case, it is the most "offended" function of

---

[93] Letter from Margrit Zwingli of 30 May 1934 (ETH Archives).

consciousness, because it is the one that is most pressed against the wall. All of these are functions of consciousness, which represent the activities of the I. At first sight, this seems a curious fact. In essence, the I consists first of memories, that is, of a certain continuity, and then of a number of very personal secrets, that is, of the so-called subjective portions or parts. Further, the I is also subject to a number of affects that it suffers.

Finally, there is another category, namely the so-called incursions or invasions from the unconscious. Already affects are in a certain sense something like incursions from the unconscious and show some of their character. They "happen" to us, and very often we are assaulted by them like in an explosion. In general, however, we are still able to exercise some control over them with the will and to explain them as sequelae to the perception of emotional reactions. The incursions, however, do not lend themselves readily to any rational explanation. As a rule, they no longer lie within the continuity of our consciousness, but instead emerge from a sphere of darkness. They arise abruptly, to our own surprise—and, if we communicate them, also to the surprise of our environment.

Under certain external circumstances, an idea with certain contents occurs to you all of a sudden, for instance, or a certain mood overcomes you, which, it seems, stands in no rational context with those external circumstances. For example, you should be concentrating on a boring lecture, but instead you playfully engage with other things, or have fantasies, which is understandable, because naturally it is nicer to play with something more amusing than the lecture. It can also happen, however, that while you are preoccupied with something of great interest to you, all of a sudden opinions, prejudices against certain people, or fantasy images appear, perhaps of a disturbing nature. Here those incursions show their autonomous character even more clearly. They can also have the character of illusions or, in very intense moments, even of hallucinations. Classic examples are Goethe's visions on his way home from Sesenheim[94] or

---

[94] Goethe described this experience in *Poetry and Truth* (1808–1831 [1848], p. 433): "Amid all this pressure and confusion I could not fail to see Frederica once more. Those were painful days, the memory of which has not remained with me. When I reached her my hand from my horse, the tears stood in her eyes, and I felt very uneasy. I now rode along the footpath towards Drusenheim, and here one of the most singular forebodings took possession of me. I saw, not with the eyes of the body, but with those of the mind, my own figure coming towards me, on horseback, and on the same road, attired in a dress which I had never worn; it was pike-grey with somewhat of gold. As soon as I shook myself out of this dream, the figure had entirely disappeared. It is strange, however, that eight years afterwards, I found myself on the very road, to pay one more visit to Frederica, in the dress of which I had dreamed, and which I wore, not from choice, but by accident."

Saul's visions on his way to Damascus.[95] This chapter naturally also includes all pathological manifestations in neuroses or psychoses.

This would be about as much as we can know about the conditions of inner perception. Thereafter comes what is innermost, of which we have no knowledge, and which we call the unconscious, the meaning of which is "that which we do not know." And yet this hypothesis is somehow called for; it is actually a postulate. We postulate it because "something emerges from it," just as people assumed there were subterranean caves because things came out of the ground. So let us assume that such a kind of cave exists. It would also be possible, however, that things emerge out of nothing, from a "no man's land."[96] It is not even possible to prove that these things exist when they are in the unconscious, for the essential character of the unconscious is that it is unknown. So when we speak of "the unconscious," we are merely using a negative boundary term, one which indicates: It is dark there. We have no knowledge of what actually happens there. We postulate, however, that the things of which we are not conscious *at this moment* somehow nevertheless exist, in the shape of memory traces, for instance, or of dispositions, which are stored like Platonic "ideas" in heaven. We can thus assume that the unconscious is a kind of Platonic heaven, where images of the things exist, and wait to become conscious. It looks as if they led an existence in the unconscious from which they walk out at the right opportunities. These are, of course, anthropomorphic notions, which we are entertaining about something that is simply unknowable.

We can now make distinctions about the kinds of things that break into consciousness, just as modern physics makes hypotheses about what happens inside the atom. These distinctions are purely hypothetical, but we have to make them so as to get an idea of these phenomena. Thus, depending on the character of things that break into consciousness, we can distinguish between personal contents, on the one hand, and collective contents, on the other.

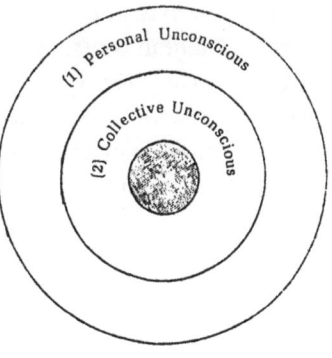

---

[95] Acts 9, 1–5. In his works, Jung repeatedly referred to the vision of Saul/Paul, the "prototype" of "miraculous conversions" (1957, § 566).

[96] This expression in English in the notes.

Personal contents are all those psychic contents that we have acquired in the course of our life, memory traces, which occasionally break into consciousness with more or less energy or "charge." So we assume there exists a certain upper layer of the unconscious that contains the personal traces.

The collective contents are fundamentally different from the personal ones, but as a rule they are very difficult to discern although they are so different from one another. Usually, they appear in such a manner that leads one to believe that they are personal memories, and only closer scrutiny reveals that their personal aspect is only a metaphor. It is as if consciousness had construed a professional language about those perceptions, or as if these collective contents had clothed themselves in such memories when piercing the personal layer. It can also happen that the person concerned identifies with this content and treats it as if it were their very personal property.

Now this is all very abstract, and I should explain it with the help of examples. In any event, present-day psychology is not yet ready to see these things in a proper light. Just recently a French scholar[97] told me that it would indeed be a very mystical idea to assume that a collective unconscious existed. I replied that I saw nothing mystical about it, for it was really a very practical idea. After all, it would be outright impossible for human beings to communicate if they had no common basis of human mental functioning. The basis of human experience is by all means the same, and that is why we can empathize with the most primitive people and, to some extent, understand their rock paintings. Our languages, too, point to common roots, and there are primordial words of humanity. On the East African coast, they also say "baba"[98] and "mama"—unfortunately, "baba" is used for mama, and vice versa. Human emotions are everywhere the same. But also in animals: If you take an apple from a monkey he will get angry exactly like a human. Through the animal part in the collective unconscious, we can reach very deep layers indeed, and can look back into infinite periods of time through these animal traces. The period of primitive man is very short compared with the animal period.

Take for instance the so-called flying dreams. You feel as if you were not flying but *swimming* in the air. Already several decades ago, this

---

[97] Possibly Lucien Lévy-Bruhl (1857–1939), whom Jung had invited to speak at the Psychological Club in Zurich around this time. On Jung and Lévy-Bruhl, cf. Shamdasani, 2003, pp. 290–293, 296–297. With thanks to Sonu Shamdasani.

[98] In German, *Papa* = daddy.

prompted a German scholar[99] to conclude that this was a memory trace of the fact that the human species had spent a long time in an amphibian state. Admittedly, the human species has probably spent the most part of its existence in an amphibian state, and that is why animal traces predominate in us, just like the possibly one-million-year-old traces of primitive prehistoric man. In the latter case we can provide even stronger evidence for them; all essential traits of the primitive are still present in us. We can see them quite clearly; we only believe they are modern.

Today, researchers still think that the primitives are so exceedingly primitive because often they cannot explain their own rites. For instance, when the sun rises, they blow or spit into their hands and hold them up to the rising sun.[100] Why do they do this? Indeed, they do not know; their fathers already did the same, and so did their grandfathers, and so forth. In such cases, one always blames the parents or grandparents, and those blame *their* parents and grandparents. Let us assume that I directed my caravan up onto the Zürichberg instead of into the African bush, and that I would study the habits of the local people in their "kraals." I would ask them: "Do you also have religious ceremonies?" "No," they would reply, "well, perhaps in bygone times!" But then one Easter morning they would come out into their gardens and do mysterious things in the bushes. We ought to ask them: "What are you doing? Do you worship hare idols, and do the eggs represent some fertility or magic ritual?" They do not know. How very primitive these people are! And the same holds true at Christmas time. Ladies and Gentlemen, it is exceedingly difficult to know what the Christmas tree means. It reaches back far into the past and has many ramifications.[101] We always assume that there was a heroic age when our forefathers knew the reason, but we deceive ourselves—they never knew. We know a thousandfold more about these matters than our ancestors. They simply did these things. They performed the strangest ceremonies, involving snakes, dragons, colorful monsters, until someone suddenly asked: "Why are we doing this?" Only after hundreds of thousands of years of just doing things did humans start to think. We are very slowly

---

[99] Perhaps a reference to Ernst Haeckel (1834–1919) and his recapitulation theory ("ontogeny recapitulates phylogeny").

[100] A ceremony of the Elgonyis (cf. Jung, 1962, p. 296).

[101] Jung liked to cite the customs of the Christmas tree and Easter eggs as examples of how Westerners, too, had come to accept archetypal images "without question and without reflection," because they "are so packed with meaning that people never think of asking what they really do mean" (1934d, § 22). Cf. Jung, 2018, p. 96.

waking up from a deep sleep of *participation mystique*,[102] a rich primordial state, in which things were lived.

We, too, still do things that we do not understand, because we have not yet fully woken up. We still live things that we have not yet thought. People do certain things when "it is thinking in them." For instance, this incredibly impressive moment when the sun rises from beneath the equator and shoots its first arrows up toward the sky. In this way we can understand sun rituals: The rising of the sun seizes people emotionally, and then they simply have to do something—although they cannot explain why. Don't they all shout with joy when they reach a mountain top in Switzerland? Or at the lido, everybody shrieks. You simply have to do something when you are allowed to expose yourself in such a risqué costume or plunge into cold water![103]

With the advent of spring, we are moved by something unknown to spring into action, and we think these traditions go back to father and mother. We put it onto our forefathers, and so we believe we have explained it. But we haven't explained it at all. The truth of the matter is that the unconscious thought—the unconscious life inside us—compels us to behave accordingly. When spring comes and everything is new and full of hope, then something must be done with it—either for or against! If one is fearful, then one must [. . .],[104] and otherwise one must arrange Easter bunnies, hide eggs, and so forth.

It is exactly the same with my Negroes. They are seized by the first ray of the sun, and then they blow and spit into their hands, and hold them up toward the rising sun. They call the human breath *roho*, which also means wind and spirit, and a dying person's last breath. Also in other languages: German *röcheln*, Hebrew *ruach*, Latin *pneuma*. The Holy Spirit is in actual fact the Holy Wind. Consequently, the Gothic Bible renders the Holy Ghost as *atu*, the breath, and in the Catholic Church the Holy Spirit is the breath that travels between the Father and the Son. Spitting alludes to a ghost, a "haunted" place.[105] Saliva is considered a substance of life that

---

[102] This expression only in Hannah (p. 112).

[103] In 1929–1930, a public swimming beach was laid out on Jung's neighboring property (Stiftung C. G. Jung Küsnacht, 2009, p. 48), causing him to have a two-meter-high wall erected between the two plots. It seems likely that Jung spoke (also) from his own experience when he talked about the noise coming from there. With thanks to Ulrich Hoerni.

[104] The ellipsis is from Sidler, who obviously did not catch what Jung said at this point. Missing in Schärf and Hannah.

[105] Untranslatable play on the words *spucken* (to spit) and *spuken* (to be haunted). There is no evidence, however, for a common etymological root of *spucken* and *spuken*.

contains *mana*. It has a healing effect. In the New Testament, Christ makes a dough out of saliva and earth to heal the blind man.[106]

When the Negroes spit into their hands and hold them up toward the rising sun, they give their soul to God, as if they wanted to say: "Into thy hands I commend my spirit."[107] God is the moment when, after this tropical night, which is so eerie and bizarre, the sun rises. The rising of the sun in those regions is an unbelievably impressive moment. There is no dawn, the day turns immediately into night, and vice versa. So this is why the appearance of light is such an incredible moment, for anything that triggers affects in us also triggers affects in the primitives. We laugh about those sensitive souls who walk up the Uetliberg[108] to see the sunrise, but when we experience it ourselves we, too, are stirred, for we, too, are human beings.

The unconscious evidently comprises psychic processes that have either already become lost to consciousness and become forgotten or ones that do not yet exist and have not yet been born. That is, they are not yet given to consciousness. Not only does the unconscious thus contain memory traces, but also traces of what is to grow and will become creative. Everything[109] springs from the collective unconscious. Many teachings of Jesus, for instance, can already be found in his cousin, Mithras. The contents of the collective unconscious—the incursions that squeeze through the personal layer—assume its mode of manifestation, that is, the qualities of personal life. This collective unconscious is a source. While it contains the memory traces of the past, it comprises at the same time the creative seeds that do not actually belong to the individual but to humanity at large. What emerges from the personal unconscious is "my business"; what emerges from the collective unconscious are matters related to humanity in general and therefore not my business in this sense.

When my Negroes greet the sun, for instance, this is a collective affair, not a matter of individual preference. And it also has a contagious effect. When they greet the new moon, for example, they make a gesture like this;[110] and then we, too, waved our hats every time. When you are standing in a crowd that is stirred up, then you are also stirred, notwithstanding all logic and insight, which counts for nothing. And you can be sure that nobody is stirred by nothing. We are always stirred by *something*.

[106] John 9, 1–7.
[107] Luke 23, 46.
[108] Zurich's "backyard" mountain, 2,851 feet above sea level.
[109] This and the following phrase only in Hannah (p. 113).
[110] The notes do not specify what gesture Jung made here.

We are also superstitious, because we are without fail affected by collective matters. So when you are standing among primitives, then you will also be stirred. You will believe and feel things that you cannot apprehend otherwise. When[111] we are in a crowd and don't understand a joke we must still laugh, because we are moved by the crowd's emotion. There's no logic to this, but it's a fact. It's no use saying this would be "nothing but" this or that; people are not moved by something that is not real. If I were not a psychologist, I'd have been lying to you about this all the time and have pretended I couldn't care less about it! But I too am moved by these things; one would not be human at all if this were not the case! One would simply be suppressing a primordial fact. This is the problem of our times. We suppress primitive thinking. We are intellectual, place ourselves above humanity, and are therefore no longer able to feel how humans have always felt.

We should not believe, however, that these things are always good and beautiful. Demonic and unfathomable evil also exists in humans, and this is almost even more contagious. It is exactly those things we repress and don't want to have that represent the danger. It is therefore good to become conscious of these things and to know that one is human, just like everyone else, feeling the very same things. Matters are not as they are described in the old textbook of the Swiss Medical Corps: "The brain is like a bowl of macaroni."[112] The unconscious is not just a container filled with various things, but a living being with a meaning and a purpose in itself. It is purposive, living, and not simply arranged along causal lines. It strives toward a goal, and it constantly seeks a way to attain this goal. The same is true of the collective unconscious. It does not seek to find your personal way, however, but the way of man, of all mankind.[113] This insight marks the beginning of the efforts of Western man to abandon the path of his narrow-minded intellectual way.

---

[111] The following passage until "nothing but" is also taken from Hannah (ibid.).

[112] Jung told the same anecdote in an interview with Stephen Black in 1955: "Joking with my pupils, I told them of an old textbook for the Medical Corps in the Swiss Army which gave a description of the brain, saying it looked like a dish of macaroni, and the steam from the macaroni was the psyche" (in McGuire & Hull, 1977, p. 262).

[113] Sidler and Schärf have: "the entire people."

Lecture 7

8 June 1934

I RECEIVED TWO questions. There is a letter waiting for one lady, which she may come and collect after today's lecture. The second question concerns the issue of the collective unconscious,[114] which I will deal with in the course of today's lecture.

* * *

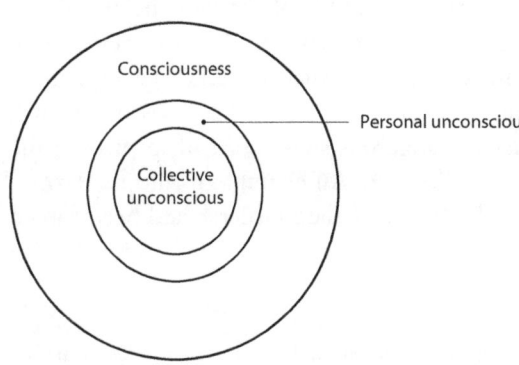

The collective unconscious is not only a *receptaculum* of the past, but also a living organism containing the future development as well as the past. The historical past casts its shadows into our souls, and even greater shadows in fact. The shadow of the future allows us to learn even more and greater things about somebody than the shadow of the past. Psychologically speaking, we move away from the past and into the future. The former is alive and reproducible in us in the form of memory. Our childhood memories are everlasting, and can break forth or be revoked at any time.

Given the power of history in man, it is even more astonishing that the future—that is, what does not yet exist—is also powerful. In the unconscious, however, it seems as if these things already somehow existed, like

---

[114] Letter of 5 June 1934 from Hans Ludger, student of architecture, asking whether there is, "besides the collective unconscious, also a collective unconscious of the race and perhaps also of the family" (ETH Archives).

a seed that is difficult to decipher. But in reality these things are not seed-like at all, but are present in their full force, although we cannot explain them. We always seek to explain matters through the past, and our attempts to do so usually fail. Consequently, there are a number of things that we cannot quite explain—unless they have already happened. Obviously, this is a very complicated and yet also highly interesting topic, namely, the creative activity of the unconscious. The organism is forever creating new goals; not from nothing, however, but from the past, specifically from the image of the past. The more prospective and stronger the things that the unconscious creates, the deeper and older the pasts are from which they have been gathered. In most cases, great creations conjure up primordial images.

The term "archetype" goes back to Augustine, and designates something like Plato's "eidola," that is, images laid down in the human soul since time immemorial.[115] These are images of typical situations, in which mankind has moved time and again. There exist mythical motifs that are prevalent among all peoples of the earth. One of the most beautiful collections in this respect can be found in Leo Frobenius's work on the myth of the sun hero.[116] The hero in general is just such an archetype. Or a more specific image would be the motif of the danger when crossing a ford. Dragons may be waiting there—dangerous snakes or evil spirits—or the hero is lured into an ambush at the ford. An example would be Parricida's murder of King Albrecht.[117] It is as if the murderer had been forced to wait until the king had invoked the typical situation by his dictum [. . .].[118]

---

[115] Cf. Jung, 1935, § 845: "Among these inherited psychic factors there is a special class which is not confined either to family or to race. These are the universal dispositions of the mind, and they are to be understood as analogous to Plato's forms *(eidola)*, in accordance with which the mind organizes its contents. One could also describe these forms as *categories* analogous to the logical categories, which are always and everywhere present as the basic postulates of reason. Only, in the case of our 'forms,' we are not dealing with categories of reason but with categories of the *imagination*. As the products of imagination are always in essence visual, their forms must, from the outset, have the character of images and moreover of *typical* images, which is why, following St. Augustine, I call them 'archetypes.'"

[116] Frobenius, 1904. Leo Frobenius (1873–1938) was a noted German ethnologist, especially known for his African studies. His book on the Sun God was variously quoted by Jung, most often in *Symbols of Transformation* (1911/12).

[117] King Albrecht I was murdered in 1308 by his nephew Johann, called Parricida (= assassin of head of state, traitor, murderer of near relative) (1290–1313), when crossing the river Reuß.

[118] So in Sidler's notes, which miss the alleged utterance of the king. There are different versions, or legends, of this incident in the literature. Jung told the story thus in *Children's*

In primitive countries, such situations become even more obvious. In the wild, it is wise to always first cross a river before setting up camp. One would rather not take the chance of swimming across, due to the crocodiles. One never knows whether a storm will break all of a sudden, causing the river to swell for days or even weeks. Crossing a river is always a special enterprise where dangers lurk. Someone might fall into the water, or baggage can be lost. You can also be attacked by another tribe in such a tight situation. This archetype thus has a very powerful effect in Africa.

There is a book by a High Commissioner, entitled *In the Shadow of the Bush*,[119] which contains an interesting story about the danger of crossing a ford. Although there was no crocodile in the water, this particular crossing was feared by the natives "because it was guarded by snake spirits." When he took this path, a cobra crossed it between himself and his wife, who was in front of him. He snatched his revolver and took a shot at it. Unfortunately, when the cobra was shot, it soared up and grazed his wife's cheek, but just as easily it could have bitten her.[120]

We are advised not to believe such stories, for surely no cobras will be guarding the Elefantenbach.[121] Other dangerous crossings, however, exist in our parts. We must not forget that we have psychological fords, narrows, and difficulties within ourselves, which may seem to be projected to another situation, as in the crossing of the Bahnhofstrasse.[122] It is quite easy to explain this rationally. But if one is psychologically in a tight spot internally, one is unable to summon enough attention and precaution externally. Then such "coincidences" may be revealing also in our parts.

Dreams: "Parricida could already have killed him before. But only when they were riding into the ford did he summon his courage: 'Why should we let ride this *Chaib* in front of us any longer' (a *Chaib* is horse carrion), and he drew his sword and killed King Albrecht" (1987 [2008], p. 150).

[119] Talbot, 1912.

[120] "One evening we reached the river bank a little before sunset. I was ahead with my gun, next came Bimba, and then my wife, followed by our botanical collector. Suddenly I heard a warning cry, and looking back saw my wife pointing to a small cobra which had crossed the path between herself and her sister. Bimba at once passed me, so as to be out of the way, and our positions then formed a triangle, with the snake, between my wife and myself, for its apex. I shot, and thought that the reptile had been blown to pieces, as it disappeared. Next moment our collector sprang into the air with a yell of terror. The cobra had been 'lofted' by the shot at a seemingly impossible angle, had hit my wife across the mouth with its tail, and then fallen just beyond her feet, in close proximity to the bare brown toes of our black companion. Almost at the same spot, an Oban man had been bitten in the heel by one of this species a few days before, and had died within the hour" (ibid., pp. 89–90).

[121] A stream running through Zurich.

[122] Zurich's main downtown street.

Among the Negroes, archetypes of the ford and others are much more touched upon, and such moods are extraordinarily powerful. On my way to a certain location on Mount Elgon, I had to cross a dense bamboo forest. The usually cooperative natives complained, "Why do you wish to continue; it is so hot and we are tired." I said, "This is ridiculous, I am a hundred years old, and you are small boys!" The corporal even dropped his rifle to show how tired he was. In the end, they had to walk right in front of me, and I followed them with my whip. They showed such signs of fear, however, that I finally whispered the magic word to the corporal, which one must not say aloud: "ghosts." Relieved he said, "Yes, indeed, there are 10,000 of them here!" I found the situation unpleasant only because we were crossing the bamboo on a rhinoceros trail. We had to make our way bent over along the unpleasantly meandering trail, trodden into the undergrowth like a tunnel a mere five feet high. At every bend we risked facing a rhinoceros with a ten-inch tusk. Dense bamboo bushes, standing perhaps eight feet tall, no rustling, and a deadly silence; a mysterious twilight, the ground covered in six inches of foliage. One has a sense of walking underwater, and one is cast into an unconscious mood. It is uncanny, the archetype of the eerie forest. Naturally, this stirs up the collective unconscious among the primitives. Their collective unconscious is much closer to the surface, whereas ours is concealed by the trivia of our culture.

Upon my arrival in Africa, someone had already said to me on the first day, "May I give you a piece of advice?" I said that I was glad to get any advice, and he replied: "You know, Sir, this isn't man's country, this is God's Country."[123] The first time you reach the African plateau, the sight of vast herds with thousands of animals and the lions around them will make a tremendous impression on you. It is a country of the Gods, in which humans play in fact a subordinate role, secondary to the elephant, the lion, the giant snake, and so on."

---

[123] In *Memories, Dreams, Reflections* (=MDR), Jung gave a more detailed account of this incident: "By the Uganda railway ... we travelled to its provisional terminus.... The boys unloaded our quantities of equipment. I sat down on a chop box ... and lit a pipe, meditating on the fact that here we had, as it were, reached the edge of the *oikumene*, the inhabited earth.... After a while an elderly Englishman, obviously a squatter, joined me, sat down, and likewise took out a pipe. He asked where we were going. When I outlined our various destinations, he asked me: 'Is this the first time you have been in Africa? I have been here for forty years,' 'Yes,' I told him. 'At least in this part of Africa.' 'Then may I give you a piece of advice? You know, mister, this here country is not man's country, it's God's country. So if anything should happen, just sit down and don't worry.' Whereupon he rose and without another word was lost in the horde of Negroes swarming around us" (1962, pp. 285–286).

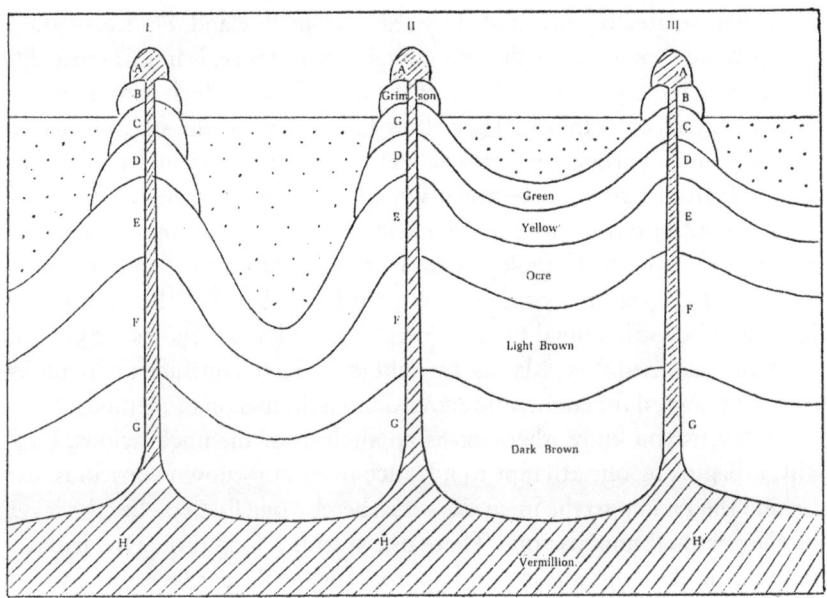

The collective unconscious is not only a very general given factor, a very general basis of humanness, which reaches back to the animal age as it were, but it also has a differentiation, as indicated in this picture.

The blue (dotted area) denotes the sea. Islands rise from it from two stories high. Uppermost are individualized persons; they are separated by the medium of the unconscious. The storey underneath is the substratum of the family. No one is alone. Everybody brings along a family. It is not you or your wife who have children, but the family itself has children, as you will realize with astonishment when you have children of your own. There exists a family unconscious, a *spiritus familiaris*, a series of family characteristics that remind people of this particular family, for instance, the Habsburg lower lip, that is, a family trait that is also accompanied by certain psychological traits. Everybody is accompanied by a kind of *spiritus familiaris*, of which they are not conscious themselves, but which is often quite obvious to others. The green designates the clan, for instance, two families that belong to the same clan. There a clan unconscious develops. The clan stratum may display a peculiarity found in a certain valley. In Switzerland, there are whole valleys where everybody is related by blood. Beneath that lies the layer of the nation, here in yellow, in the sense of an enlarged valley population. Good examples of this layer are countries that are either isolated or surrounded by sea, such as England, France, or Italy. The psychic experience of the Frenchman, for instance, is in this sense different from the psychic experience of the Englishman, which you can prove with hundreds of examples. The yellow-brown layer is the stratum shared by everyone in Europe, for example, that is, the European in distinction to someone from East Asia, between whom there are profound differences. Many people are convinced that we will never be able to understand Chinese psychology. The Chinese possess neither the European form of experience nor European dispositions. Even further below lies the anthropoid layer, and beneath animal life in general. The red area denotes the central fire that has raised these islands. I would thus like to conclude my remarks on psychological functions, and move on to a discussion of methods.

Today, as you know, there exists an analysis of the unconscious. Usually, it begins by our attempt to advance from our known consciousness behind the I and into the unconscious, whereby one first reaches the layer of the personal unconscious. There one spends a long time. One usually turns around on the surface, and approaches the deeper layers in a spiral fashion. This involves the danger of losing oneself in this maze, walking around in circles, and discovering nothing but the personal. This is because the relatively broad and trodden roads stay on the outside, whereas the footpaths that lead inward are nearly impossible to find. Then you come into the collective unconscious. Here, too, you may go round in circles for a very long time, simply moving in archaic representations without reaching the center. The complexes of the personal unconscious, erected upon primordial images of human behavior, are so to speak individual variations of general motifs. One is easily inclined to remain circling in the personal variants without arriving at the typical. Once one enters the typical, the entire matter unfolds on a different track. This is difficult to grasp, and I may return to this subject later.

The methods refer to this problem of penetrating into the unconscious. For these inner occurrences mostly elude a conscious approach, not only by the observer, but also by the individual person. We must find some ways in which to bring these inner matters into a constellation so that we can grasp them at all. As a rule, one is quite explicitly averse to becoming involved with one's own background. It is considered unhealthy to brood over oneself. "Normal people don't brood over their motives," but simply get on with life in a "fresh, pious, cheerful, and free" manner.[124] One

---

[124] *Frisch, fromm, fröhlich, frei* was the motto of German gymnasts, popularized by "*Turnvater*" Jahn (1778–1852), and later instrumentalized by the Nazis.

can obviously indulge in one's own neurosis, but the study of man is also a legitimate enterprise. After all, the human being is the noblest task of science, towering above all its other tasks. It is the highest and most interesting task, in my unauthoritative opinion.

The simplest method is the method of association. I will first show you the experiment in detail. It consists in calling out the stimulus word to the test person, requesting them to utter as quickly as possible the first word that crosses their mind, namely, with reference to the meaning of the stimulus word, and not to its tone or sound. For practical reasons, it suffices to measure the differences under consideration in fifths of a second; greater accuracy is of no use. The association experiment is conducted with a series of words. After the experiment, in the so-called reproduction experiment, the test person is asked in each instance what their original response was, so as to see if they remember their first reaction to the word in question; "+" stands for yes, "–" for no. A "complex-characteristic" denotes a disturbance, for instance, when the test person hesitates, says "oh," repeats the stimulus word, associates "cold" to "water," or answers with two words instead of one, and so on. Here is an example:

	Reaction Time	Complex-Characteristics	Reproduction
1. Water	4/5	0	+
2. Round	4/5	0	+
3. Chair	5/5	0	+
4. Swimming	6/5	0	+
5. Grass	5/5	0	+
6. Blue	7/5	0	+
7. *Knife*	20/5	3	–
8. To help	15/5	3	–
9. Weight	10/5	1	–
10. Finished	8/5	0	+
11. Mountain	6/5	1	–
12. To fly	5/5	0	+

With the twelfth answer, the normal level has been reattained. These are twelve out of the one hundred stimulus words that were used. Between answers 7 and 11, we observe a period of disturbances. Later, there will be still other such perseverations. After the word "sharp," there was a reaction time of 15/5 seconds, and the answer was not recollected in the reproduction either. I did not know the test person, a thirty-five-year-old man. I asked him, "Did you notice that you sometimes hesitated when giving an answer?" "No, I was always able to answer promptly." So he was completely unaware of those disturbances. "Did certain memories occur as you were answering?" "No." I then drew his attention to the fact that disturbances occurred with this and that word. Suddenly he starts blushing. He is feeling uncomfortable, he becomes evasive, and wants to back out. In the end, it emerges that there is something dark in his previous history. He had lived abroad for a longer period, and had spent six months in jail because he had seriously injured someone in a knife fight. It is a most embarrassing memory to him. He is a respectable man, and nobody knows of this incident—he's got "a skeleton in the cupboard."[125] This is his complex. Thus one adopts this method if one wishes to enter into someone's personal business for professional reasons. Had I asked him directly if anything bothered him, he would have answered "no." After all, he had long wanted to forget that this ever happened. Thank goodness this episode has long been buried and forgotten. No one knows about it. And yet this is not true. It stands there forever, ready to erupt at the slightest provocation. Whenever someone uses the word "knife," for instance, he hesitates, and his eye flickers.

---

[125] This expression in English in the notes.

Lecture 8

15 June 1934

Last time, I began discussing association experiments. Today I have brought along a sheet containing the stimulus words. The case that I described last time concerned, as you will recall, a normal man, who would have later preferred to have forgotten his experience. People have all kinds of possible attitudes toward their complexes. Some are to a large extent conscious of their complexes, others prefer to forget them, and indeed others are unconscious of them to the point of amnesia.

Now I would like to cite a second example. I was once asked by an elderly gentleman, a scholar, to show him the experiment. He lived abroad, and I visited him at his place. After about seventeen reactions, the old gentleman became impatient: "Can't you tell me something about it? How should anything come out of this? This is nothing!" It was really far too early to draw definitive conclusions, but I consented as he was an old man. So I replied: "Well, with your kind permission, I will try to tell you something about it." He was about seventy, and it was clear to the trained doctor's eye that the gap separating him from the cold grave had become fairly narrow.

Of the seventeen reactions, five involved a prolonged reaction time. And so I could tell him:

1. "You are afraid of dying of a heart condition."
2. "You have financial difficulties."
3. "Strangely, you have sweet memories of a certain lady who spoke French." At first he pretended that he could not remember any such woman, but then an expression laden with memory clouded his face, and I saw that I had hit the nail on the head.

Here are his reactions:

1. "money"—"little." Someone would have to be a fool not to have noticed something here.

2. "paying"—"la semeuse,"[126] following a very long response time. So there has to be a female figure on his mind.
3. "death"—"to die."
4. "heart"—"to stab." This is the case with angina pectoris, that is, the arteriosclerosis of certain arteries.
5. "kissing"—a very long reaction time, and then he said with plainly visible feeling: "beautiful." I added two and two together. He had studied in Paris, which I did not know at the time.

This erotic memory in the late autumn of life is also quite interesting in psychological terms. It belongs in the chapter of the great recapitulation that old people must undertake to be properly prepared.

The third example concerns the case of a well-known and learned psychologist. After twenty responses, the same impatience [as in the previous case] set in: "What is this supposed to prove?" Three out of the twenty responses came with a long reaction time, and on every occasion he uttered the word "fear," and not always in a meaningful context. "You are afraid." "No! I'm never afraid!" "Well, who then is afraid?" And that is where matters stopped, because you cannot, of course, prove anything to a person who is reluctant to admit anything. It is entirely against my principles to force people to admit anything against their own determination, but by all the rules of the art it was perfectly clear that he was terribly afraid, and that his conception of himself as a public man was more important to him than the recognition of his own fear. In a public position, it is expected of one that one should never be intimidated, so he kept his fear complex a secret, even from himself.

The fourth example also concerns a person afflicted by neurosis and who was unwilling to acknowledge the fact. This person was a lady, aged thirty, whose husband consulted me, requesting that I examine his wife. So I saw the wife afterward, but got very little out of her. She said it was stupid of her husband to have consulted a psychologist, as she did not wish to discuss her psychology. Hers was a dreadful story from the beginning, because she was terribly jealous. According to the husband, he could not understand his wife at all, because he would give her no reason whatsoever to be jealous. And indeed, his looks did not give her any grounds for jealousy! In addition, he was Protestant, and she a practicing Catholic. Both maintained, however, that this made no difference. She was inordinately prudish. In the evenings, before bedtime, she would always

---

[126] French, the soweress, a figure on the reverse side of some French coins.

undress in another room. In her presence, one was not allowed to mention that her sister had a child, since this would allude to something indecent. "Otherwise it is a very happy marriage." The lady, too, confirmed that their marriage was extremely happy. She also confirmed that she was very jealous without any reason. It would pass. But this situation had already lasted for three years! She was utterly unwilling to admit that there was something pathological about this. I suggested to her to conduct an association experiment.

1. The first word that produced a disturbance was "yellow"—"envy." She then said: "yellow with envy."[127] "Why are you yellow with envy?" "Envy of the husband who might possibly do what I can't do on moral grounds."
2. "praying"—"religion." The confessional difference became apparent.
3. "separating"—elicited the thought the marriage could be dissolved.
4. "marriage"—she thought she had married the wrong man.
5. "arguing"—with her husband, of course.
6. "family"—her family should be dissolved.
7. "happiness"—no happiness in her marriage.
8. "wrong"—fantasies of an erotic character, and of affairs with other men. As a good Catholic she could not even admit the possibility of ever pursuing such a course herself, so she had projected it onto her husband, and was always imagining that he was carrying out with other women the fantasies which she had of other men, and so reacted with violent jealousy.
9. "kissing"—not her husband.
10. "choosing"—one could also choose differently.
11. "content" was also disturbed.

At the end of the experiment, she burst into tears, and all her inhibitions were broken through. We were confronted with a clear truth. In such cases, the experiment can be of great service.

The fifth example concerns a very pathological case, a thirty-two-year-old lady who was admitted to the clinic for depression. She had been given a somewhat scary diagnosis, namely a so-called catatonic depression. Its prognosis is unpleasant insofar as such patients, if they are cured, which happens once in a while, suffer a certain defect, namely an atrophy of

---

[127] *gelb vor Neid*—the English idiom would be "green with envy."

feeling, so that more subtle feelings are somehow deadened. So the outlook was pretty bleak. I could only confirm the diagnosis, and yet I sensed that there was more to the matter than met the eye.[128] I couldn't find out anything by direct questioning, and so I suggested the experiment to her.

She was married and had had two children; the older child, however, had died at the age of four, and after the death of this child the present condition had set in. We could say that this event in itself would be enough grounds for a psychoneurosis. It was not a profound mourning, however, but a pathological condition that is not induced by normal suffering, as caused by the death of a relative. We know from experience that such conditions occur if the experience has a "double floor," that is, if other—unconscious—experiences enter into the equation.

1. In the association experiment, the first word causing a disturbance was "angel." To this she of course associated her deceased daughter, who had been her darling favorite child.
2. The second word was "defiant." Here, no response whatsoever occurred. It became clear eventually that she related this word to herself, specifically to an incomprehensible, defiant stance—both after but also already before the death of her child. She could not account for this.
3. "evil"[129]—again a strong disturbance, which also related to this stance.
4. "blue"—here, she remembered her child's blue eyes. Curiously, the response time here was very short, but this was followed by the word "red," which prompted an incredible disturbance. Then we come to the critical reaction:
5. "bread"—in the experiment, this was an indifferent term, but there was a great disturbance hidden behind it. It often happens that the actual "complex stimulus word" is passed over smoothly, but that then the [reaction to the] next word is disturbed.
6. "rich"—this showed many complex characteristics and strong perseverations. This word referred to a certain rich gentleman. At this point, a part of the patient's life history began to emerge.

---

[128] There is a detailed report about this lady and Jung's ongoing treatment of her, in 1907, in his letter to Freud of 10 October 1907 (Freud & Jung, 1974, pp. 92–93), with further details, e.g., her "transference to me because of my brown eyes and tall figure" and a "sudden outburst of wild sexual excitement which quieted down after a few hours" (p. 92), but without mentioning the bathing scene. He also described this case at some length in 1962, pp. 135–138.

[129] *böse*—bad, evil.

Before marrying her husband, she had had a youthful crush on a very rich man. Her well-to-do, middle-class parents laughed at her about it, and kept telling her that she was deluding herself with the idea that she could ever mean anything to such a rich and important man. She thus put him out of her mind. But she could not quite get over him, and it rankled her that she had not managed to get to him.

7. "morals"—this, too, was followed by a strong disturbance. After a long pause: "immoral." This referred again to her defiant, nasty, and immoral mood. She admitted to having had erotic fantasies about that man, but on the other hand she also had a very strong non-erotic complex. I was dumbfounded and did not know what this could refer to.

8. "money"—here, she reacted again with a memory of that wealthy man.

9. "marriage"—now it turned out that while she got along very well with her husband, she found it difficult at first to forget her sweetheart.

She then had a child, and when she looked into its eyes after birth, she recognized the eyes of her former beloved in them. She now had the idea that the heavens had given her this child as a replacement for her lost love, and therefore she doted on it very greatly. Two years later, she gave birth to a boy, and then disaster struck. When she told me about the child, I wanted to know everything. "What did the child die from?" "Typhoid fever." She was living abroad at the time, in a region where the quality of water was doubtful, so that the drinking water and utility water pipelines were separate. She had bathed her child in this undrinkable water, and it had evidently swallowed some of this water and died.

I asked her whether she had ever seen this other man again. "No," she replied, she would have put him completely out of her mind. Then something suddenly occurred to her, namely that a friend of this man's had visited her before the death of her child. At first her husband was present, but when he left the room, the visitor told her: "You have also pierced someone to the heart with your marriage!"—meaning her former sweetheart. She said that she had nearly fainted. Then, when she was bathing her child, it was sucking the sponge. She saw this happen, yet did not stop her, and simply took her out of the bathtub. The boy then cried out that he was thirsty, and she gave the boy this water to drink. But it was the older child who then died of typhoid. Obviously, I then knew why she had this pathological depression, although she herself had no knowledge of the causal connection.

Then I thought, well, she has a bad prognosis anyway. If she were left in this state, she would degenerate, as so often happens in such cases. Finally, I took heart and said: "Have you realized that you wanted to murder these children, and at least managed to kill your favorite child?" She then broke down, but at least in a normal fashion. Within three weeks, she could be discharged as "cured." There had never been a relapse, even though this occurred twenty-five years ago.[130] I am convinced that, without a thorough analysis, I would have never found out otherwise.

The association experiment can be combined with other means, which allow one to detect feelings; for example, the psychogalvanic experiment.[131]

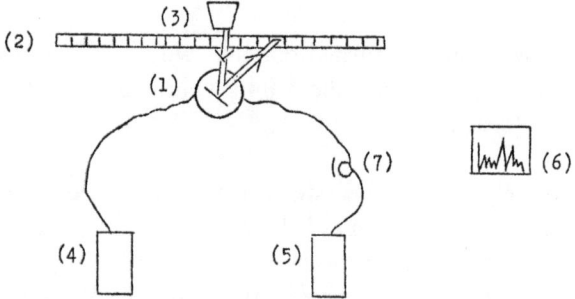

The diagram is a schematic drawing of a mirror galvanometer (1), above which is a translucent celluloid scale (2) with a lamp (3) upon it. The electrodes are usually two brass plates (4 and 5),[132] which are slightly concave, and upon which the palms of the test person are placed with light sand-bags on the backs to weigh them down. These plates are connected with a Bunsen cell (7), from which the conduit goes to the galvanometer. The nervous contractions of the skin under the test word make the mirror oscillate, and a ray of light travels along the scale above. The

---

[130] In *MDR*, Jung wrote that this happened in his early years at the Burghölzli, when he "was still a young man . . . , a beginner" (1962, p. 136), thus probably some thirty plus years before this lecture.

[131] The illustrations and the description of the galvanometer are taken from Hannah (pp. 120–121), who gives the clearest specification and probably also profited from Jung's input. For a more detailed description of the apparatus and the experiment, see Jung, 1907a; Jung & Peterson, 1907; Jung & Ricksher, 1907/08.

[132] So in Sidler, Schärf, and Hannah. In an original publication (Jung & Peterson, 1907, § 1045), Jung mentioned that he used "copper plates."

result is recorded on a rotating drum (6), on which the deflection can be read.

One calls out a stimulus word to the test subject, and registers all emotional reactions, of which the person is as a rule unaware. When a complex is touched upon, the electrical resistance of the skin decreases and more electricity passes through. These phenomena coincide with the complex characteristics, for instance, a prolonged reaction time. The person in the following chart had a highly excitable nature and showed an electrical reaction at nearly every word.

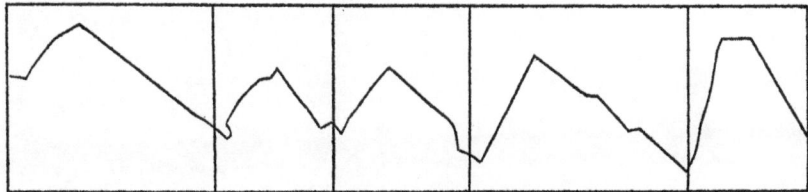

I then set up a second experiment to record the breathing curve at the same time. In the case of strong emotional responses because of a complex, a contraction of the breathing volume occurs, a certain feeling of tension in the thorax. Perhaps you are familiar with this, a tense feeling of expectation. If you are anxious about something, you will feel this particular pressure. The following drawing shows the resistivity in the case of successive complex characteristics, with the breathing volume showing a strong contraction in each instance.

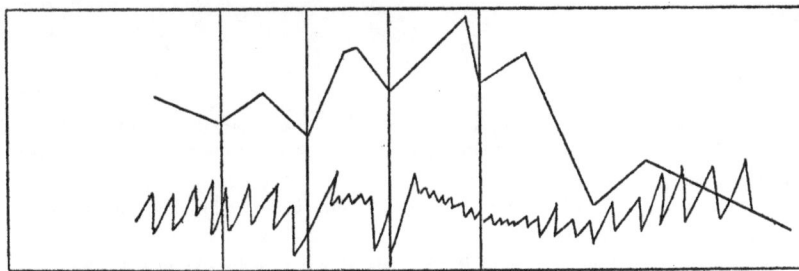

I observed cases in which the breathing was contracted throughout most of the experiment. Neurotics often breathe poorly—that is, their breath is too shallow. From time to time they have to catch up with their breathing, and heave a sigh. Now these things are often habitual with neurotics, in that they cannot breathe properly. One would think that people should at least be able to breathe normally, but even this is a problem!

Sometimes, the lungs do not receive enough air, with very unpleasant consequences. The contracted breathing volume due to chronic complexes can lead to lung apex diseases and tuberculosis. This is why lung tuberculosis is very often associated with psychogenic conditions, to the extent that in many cases tuberculosis can be said to be a psychogenic illness. Certain tuberculosis cases can therefore be cured with psychic treatment.[133] Thus, physical illnesses can be linked to psychic states in unexpected ways.

---

[133] Although Jung was certainly aware of the fact that Robert Koch (1843–1910) had discovered the tubercle bacillus in 1882 (for which he received the Nobel Prize in 1905), Jung continued to believe in a strong psychic component: "Very early on, at the time of my association experiments, I became interested in tuberculosis as a possible psychic disease, having observed that reactions due to complexes frequently cause a long-lasting reduction in the volume of breathing. This inhibition causes defective ventilation of the apices of the lungs and may eventually give rise to an infection. The shallow breathing due to complexes is often characterized by repeated deep expirations (sighs). I also observed that a large number of my neurotic patients who were tubercular were 'freed' from their complexes under psychotherapeutic treatment, learnt to breathe properly again and in the end were cured. As a result I jokingly called tuberculosis a 'pneumatic disease,' seeing that psychic relief brings about a radical change of mental attitude. I am therefore entirely of your opinion that a salutary dose of psychology should be administered not only to tubercular patients but to many others as well, and also to so-called normal people" (letter to J.A.F. Swoboda, 23 January 1960; Jung, 1976, p. 533).

Lecture 9

22 June 1934

ONE LADY WROTE to inquire about the case we talked about last time, of the woman who suffered the misfortune with her child. The lady wishes to know what happened after the woman had more or less voluntarily made her confession, up until her discharge from the clinic. Naturally all kinds of things happened, but these are matters I am not at liberty to talk about, both because it belongs to professional secrecy and because it is too specialized a field for the general public.

One gentleman would like me to expound further on the terms "extraverted and "introverted," and also about "anima" and "animus." It is quite true that the question of extraversion and introversion could have been handled with the functions, but these are very complicated concepts, and we can discuss them fruitfully only after having talked about the concept of "libido," and after gaining a bit more profound insight into the life of the unconscious. These psychological types are not meant to serve the purpose of labeling individuals, like "You now belong to the introverted tribe," etc., but they are a critical apparatus for the discovery of empirical psychological materials. While Kretschmer's types,[134] for instance, allow us to classify types, they are not suited to a strictly logical psychology. For now, such questions are still among the more advanced matters, and we will discuss them at a later stage.

---

[134] Ernst Kretschmer (1888–1964), a German psychiatrist. He had been Jung's predecessor as president of the International General Medical Society for Psychotherapy, from which he resigned on 6 April 1933. Jung then accepted the acting presidency and editorship of the society's journal, the *Zentralblatt für Psychotherapie* (see the "Chronology" in this volume). Kretschmer's classification system was based on three main body types: asthenic/leptosomic (thin, small, weak), athletic (muscular, large-boned), and pyknic (stocky, fat). Each of these body types was associated with certain personality traits and, in a more extreme form, psychopathologies. This typology was popular at the time, but is no longer influential in personality theory.

The same applies to the second question, concerning the anima. I would not like to offer you simply a discussion of terms. It is, as you perhaps know, the great difficulty of contemporary psychological science that it does not know what to do with psychological terms, quite simply because it lacks the corresponding empirical material. I would now like to show you how exactly we arrive at this material. A special method is needed for this, and you can't make these experiences without applying this method.[135] I have been accused of the most incredible things, for instance that I practice demonology and so forth. This is so stupid that one actually feels disgusted. So it is principally out of respect for my audience that I am so guarded in using these terms.

* * *

In the last lecture, I explained to you how one can more or less accurately determine emotional states. Today, I would like to talk about another application of the association experiment. If this experiment actually allows us to determine existing complexes, it should be possible to reverse matters and, for instance, use the experiment to artificially detect, so to speak, a presupposed complex in a person, in other words, to deliberately reveal a certain complex that a given person has, and knows about. This is called the [psychological] diagnosis of evidence [*Tatbestandsdiagnostik*].[136] Let us suppose that someone committed murder. In this case, he must of course have a corresponding complex, and it must be possible—if the matter holds water—to verify that complex through the experiment.

I once conducted an experiment together with Professor Zürcher.[137] We staged a mock crime, so to speak, in order to see if I could find out the "culprit." I cut a photograph out of the *Illustrirte* [sic] *Zeitung*,[138] showing an artist painting a picture with a cow and some human beings watching

---

[135] A point repeatedly made by Jung before, e.g., with regard to Freud's critics: "Freud could be refuted only by one who has made repeated use of the psychoanalytic method. . . . He who does not or cannot do this should not pronounce judgment on Freud; else he acts like those notorious men of science who disdained to look through Galileo's telescope" (1907a, Preface).

[136] Cf. Jung 1905a, 1905b.

[137] Emil Zürcher (1850–1926), after 1890 full professor of criminal law (*Strafrecht*) and law of criminal procedure (*Strafprozessrecht*) at the University of Zurich. He played an important role in preparing the Swiss penal code (Gagliardi, 1938, pp. 838–839). This example is mostly taken from Hannah (p. 122), who has the most detailed account.

[138] Modeled after the *Illustrated London News* and the Parisian *L'Illustration*, the *Illustrirte Zeitung* was the first and a highly successful illustrated German magazine, and appeared for more than a century (1843–1944).

him. Professor Zürcher selected two[139] students, of whom one was shown the picture, while the other was not. They were both sent to me so I should discover the "guilty" one, that is, the one who had seen the picture. The student with no knowledge of the picture had evidently received instructions to act a bit strangely in order to make me suspect he was the "culprit," but all critical stimulus words went past him unnoticed. The professor had chosen the best actor among the students to see the picture in the hope that he could outwit me, but all the same he was taken in by all critical stimulus words, such as cow, painter, picture, etc., which I had mixed with a lot of irrelevant words.

If it is a matter of an actual, indictable theft, then things are more critical. I have managed to solve thefts in this way, and students of mine have done likewise in Europe and America. I would like to present such a case in practical detail, namely of a theft that occurred at the Burghölzli clinic.[140] In a room in which three wardresses were sleeping, various items had been stolen from the wardrobe, including cash, a purse, and a silver watch chain. The wardrobe contained the following: laundry, a fur boa, a red leather purse containing a fifty-franc note and a twenty-franc gold piece, as well as a receipt from the Dosenbach shoe store.[141] The theft was discovered in the evening and reported to me in the morning by the head wardress. It turned out that she knew about the sum of money stolen and thus had perhaps committed the theft herself, even though she reported it. This would have been an excellent joke! The room was also occupied by the victim of the theft and a friend of the head wardress. I indicated the friend of the head wardress by the letter A, the head wardress herself by the letter B, and the third nurse, the victim, by the letter C. There was still another wardress, D, who did not sleep in the room but was charged with cleaning it. In addition, about five other wardresses had access to the room and might also have been the culprits. On the morning of the critical day, A was still lying in bed in the room. She had not been feeling well and had been given permission to stay in bed until lunchtime. The theft was discovered at dinnertime. The key to the wardrobe was hanging in view, and the room was generally accessible.

I asked A, B, and C to come to me and undergo the experiment. B knew why I was conducting it, but not the others. I included a number of

---

[139] In Sidler: four.
[140] Jung described this case at length in 1910 [1909], §§ 957–981.
[141] The Dosenbach shoe store was founded in 1865 and is still in business today.

typical words among the stimulus words: wardrobe, door, key, purse, bank notes, money, 70, 50, 20, money-bag, chain, silver, to hide, stamp, receipt, Dosenbach, and so on. In such cases I usually also mix in some scarecrow words, such as theft, disgrace, syringe, police, to arrest, innocent, etc., which are quite juicy allusions.

During the experiment, B was very agitated, but A and C remained quiet. Afterward, B had a pulse of 125,[142] so that I thought: "Well, maybe *she* was the thief after all?" I suspended judgment, however, until I had calculated matters, because innocent people also can become agitated.

In all such calculations of complexes one first calculates the probable mean reaction time for each test person.[143] Different people have different reaction times, for instance, educated persons usually a slightly shorter one than uneducated ones, not because uneducated people think more slowly, but because they become more agitated, and thus inhibited, during such an experiment.

In our case the mean reaction times were as follows:

A: 10/5 seconds,
B: 12/5 seconds,
C: 13/5 seconds.

Now there is nothing we can say about this at first. We must take a look at the relation between this probable mean and the reaction times to critical, post-critical, and indifferent stimulus words.

	A	B	C
Indifferent	10	11	12
Critical	16	13	15
Post-critical	10	11	13
Critical minus indifferent	6	2	3

---

[142] So in Sidler; Hannah has "120."
[143] Jung specified (in 1905c, §§ 571) that he did not apply the arithmetical mean but the median (or "probable mean," in Kraepelin's term), because in the former "the high values influence the otherwise quite low average values in a most disturbing and possibly quite misleading manner. This can be avoided by using the method of the probable mean, which consists in arranging the figures in the order of their numerical value and taking that nearest the middle. By this means the influence of excessively high values is eliminated."

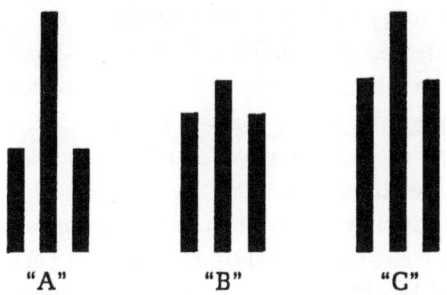

"A" "B" "C"

It is remarkable that all three persons showed prolonged reaction times with the critical stimulus words. This is mainly because they all had an inkling what this was about. It is conspicuous, however, that A showed the longest reaction time in her responses to the critical words (16), but on the other hand had the lowest value for the probable mean (10). If we take the differences between those two values, we have a difference of 6 with A, 2 with B, and 3 with C.

Now a prolonged reaction time is of course only one of the indicators. There are others, such as various displays of uncertainty, facial expressions, etc., all of which also have to be noted down and counted. In addition, we find so-called disturbances in reproduction, when we ask people after the initial experiment, "How did you originally respond to this stimulus word?," determining the person with the greatest number of memory lapses. There is still another way of determining complexes, based on the fact that disturbances in reproduction occur not only with regard to critical reactions, but often also with regard to the following reactions, thus perseverating, or even to the previous ones. If you have a head injury and pass out, you will have retrograde amnesia afterward for a half or full hour before the accident, and also anterograde amnesia that stretches for some time from the accident into the present. You speak and act quite normally, but it turns out that you have forgotten all about the ten, twenty, or thirty hours after the shock. Only then does your memory kick in once more.

When a complex acutely manifests itself, there will also be some small amnestic disturbance—a temporary obfuscation of memory—so that you no longer remember afterward what you thought after the complex shock. You may be unconscious of this shock, but it still has an amnestic effect. Each stirring up of a complex is simply a shock that always produces such a memory disturbance. This disturbance can affect up to four or more reproductions. So computing such series of disturbances in reproduction provides us with another indicator of the intensity of the complexes. The results in our case are 64.7 percent for A, 55.5 percent for B, and 30 percent for C, which is still a bit high, but approaches the normal level. This provided sufficient evidence to tell wardress A straight to her face: "You stole those items, so don't get any fancy ideas, and out with the truth!" On this note, she confessed without more ado.

Once I was consulted by a distraught guardian who suspected his adolescent ward of having stolen a "shooting thaler."[144] The guardian had heard that I would be able to elicit confessions in hypnosis. "It doesn't quite work like this," I told him, "but I'll make an experiment with him." And in fact, everything was then revealed.[145]

Thus we possess an important experiment to furnish circumstantial evidence. The matter is very delicate, however, and it is quite easy to do this in an absolutely stupid way. Of course, nothing will work if you do it stupidly. You wouldn't even be able to take a photo! The difficulty is that not only the culprit but also everyone else is acquainted with the facts of the preliminary investigation. One would need to conduct the experiment right at the outset, that is, when the majority of people have no knowledge of the facts of the case. We once had such a case at the Federal Forestry Administration [*Eidgenössische Forstverwaltung*]. The person concerned behaved so stupidly that it was immediately apparent that only he could be the culprit.

Until now, we have only discussed the use of the association experiment for the discovery of complexes. There is, however, another quite different use of the association experiment. If one determines *how* people react in a purely formal manner, it becomes apparent that there are very different types of human beings. For instance, there are persons who have a strange preference for adjectives, or for judgments, or others who have purely linguistic, motor reactions. So I have devised a schema to categorize responses in logical and linguistic terms. The application of this schema gives us specific percentages for the qualities of association. Comparison with other types then allows us to determine certain reaction types.[146]

---

[144] A *Schützentaler* ("shooting thaler") is a coin, often of considerable value, minted to commemorate one of the traditional yearly *Schützenfeste* (marksmen's festivals) held in various cantons of Switzerland, and awarded as a shooting prize.

[145] Jung cited this as the case in which he "succeeded for the first time in testing out, on a delinquent, our method of discovering complexes" (1905a, § 481), and described it at more length in 1905b, §§ 769–775.

[146] These researches led to the first nucleus of Jung's typology. He and Franz Riklin (1904/05) had found that "some individuals tend to react with internal associations and others with external ones." In other words, "two easily recognizable types emerge: (1) A type

This procedure is mainly used for studying family psychology. The latter is extraordinarily important, because we all come from a family and everyone once, unconsciously, rested in its bosom. The family is like an atmosphere, like the mother's bosom, in which we were all once secure as infants, and were consequently in an unconscious state. When we are still in a relatively unconscious state, we are also in a primitive state of mind. In primitives, this condition lasts a lifetime. Not only are they semiconscious or conscious only to a very limited degree, but it also follows that this lacking consciousness results in insufficient discrimination. Only when I realize that I am different from others am I conscious of myself. When I am not sufficiently conscious of myself, I won't even be able to tell the difference between myself and this table! Distinguishing differences is the nature of consciousness. It is therefore said that discrimination is the essential quality of consciousness.

When human beings live unconsciously, they live in a condition of non-differentiation. They live in this strange state that Levy-Bruhl called *participation mystique*,[147] that is, in a participation in the lives of others, and indeed in a non-differentiation from the others' lives. We call it "mystique," mystical, because we fail to understand it; after all, we call everything mystical that we do not understand. And the reason we don't understand it is because we are still stuck in it. Insofar as we are still unconscious, we are involved in the *participation mystique*. In all matters in which we share unconsciousness, we are not yet distinct from one another. The most striking example is that we always assume that others should think and feel in the same way as we do. "What I like, others also like." As a matter of fact, we always tend to presuppose a similar state of affairs in others. People blather, throwing explanations over the others' heads, and think they understand each other. Such thinking is really pathetic. It would be much more sincere to think: Nobody understands anyone else! The claim that "we are all the same" leads to the most incredible acts of violence against others. It is not to the credit of a culture, for instance, if it makes

---

in whose reactions subjective, often feeling-toned experiences are used. (2) A type whose reactions show an objective, impersonal tone. . . . This type can be called objective" (ibid., § 382, 412). So his first classification distinguished between "subjective" and "objective" types. Cf. Falzeder, 2016.

[147] Jung repeatedly referred to Lévy-Bruhl's notion of *participation mystique*, or mystical participation, e.g.: "It denotes a peculiar kind of psychological connection with objects, and consists in the fact that the subject cannot clearly distinguish himself from the object but is bound to it by a direct relationship which amounts to partial identity" (Jung, 1921, Definitions, no. 40; cf. 2018, p. 95). On 9 February 1935, Lévy-Bruhl gave a lecture, entitled "L'experience mythique chez le primitives," at the Psychological Club in Zurich, and again, on 13 February 1935, at the University of Zurich.

no distinctions between people; on the contrary, this is a sign of non-culture. It is not mean-spirited toward others to find that they are different. We can only be fair-minded by making distinctions. What is good for me is bad for the other. We can only do justice to others by realizing that we are different from one another. Through this unconscious non-differentiation from our parents and grandparents, from our siblings, and even from cats and dogs, we take part in the entire family to such an extent that we are deeply affected by it for a long time. If we remain unconscious of it, this state will continue, for what is unconscious is not subject to correction. Only consciousness corrects. You can only change something by making it conscious. In consciousness, there is fighting and friction; it is the place where rules can be softened and errors corrected.

Consequently, it is most important to establish the "*spiritus familiaris*." One can do this by determining the habitual reaction of a family. This is done by categorizing reactions according to their qualities, using a scheme that I will present next time. There are fifteen different qualities. To find out the family type, we take all the results—depending on the number of family members—and determine their arithmetic mean, which in turn gives us the average family type. From this average type, we can establish the deviation of single individuals. We often find that it is precisely the most nervous and deranged family members that come closest to the family type and are the most affected by it. Here is an example of such a *participation mystique* between husband and wife:

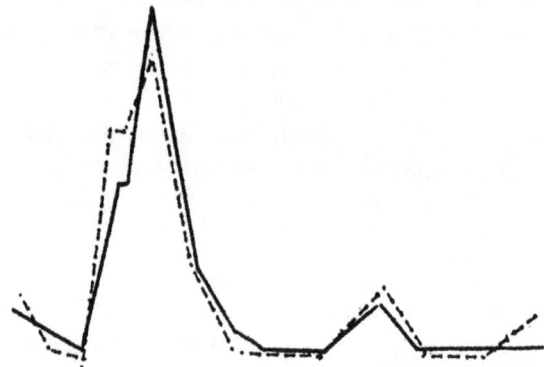

This diagram is the chart of such a test applied to a husband and wife.[148] (The black line is the husband and the broken line the wife.) It will be

---

[148] This paragraph is only in Hannah (p. 125).

observed how very closely the lines follow each other; this is because the two are in *participation mystique* with each other. They have both been very much bound up in their families and carried over this attitude, even calling each other "Papa" and "Mama." Probably both families had had this attitude in an unbroken line since the fourteenth century.

Lecture 10

29 June 1934[149]

Let us proceed with our investigation of family psychology. Here is a list of fifteen reaction qualities, which will help us to group the reactions:

1. Coordination; a logical attribution.
2. Sub- and supraordination: house—village; town—houses; blue—colors.
3. Contrast.
4. Predicates expressing a personal judgment. These are often favored by elderly women; for example: winter—wonderful; going for a walk—boring.
5. Simple predicates, that is, analogous matter-of-fact predicates: water—green.
6. Relations of the verb to the subject or complement: roses—bloom.
7. Designations of time, place, etc.: warm—summertime; sleep—at night; dark—in the basement.
8. Definitions: chair—furniture; cow—mammal. These associations are especially prevalent with persons with an intelligence complex, and are not entirely certain whether or not others consider them stupid. There are cases in which definitions account for 90–100 percent of the associations. These are truly imbeciles; there is no doubt whatsoever that such persons are really dumb.
9. Coexistence: table—chair; flower—window; hand—foot.

---

[149] Sidler's notes for this lecture are missing. He noted a week later: "I skipped last week's lecture. (Mountain hike ... with Ernst Wildhaber)." The lecture mostly recapitulates Jung's second talk at Clark University in 1909 (Jung, 1909), which in itself is nearly identical with an earlier article (Jung, 1907b). The material is based on investigations carried out by Emma Fürst (1875–1939), Jung's collaborator at the time at the Burghölzli. She had "applied the association experiment to twenty-four families, consisting altogether of one hundred subjects. The resulting material amounted to 22,200 associations.... Fifteen clearly defined groups were formed according to logical-linguistic criteria and the associations were arranged" accordingly (Jung, 1909, §§ 999–1000).

10. Identity: walk—go on foot; room—chamber.
11. Linguistic associations: free—freedom; book—books.
12. Compound words:[150] table—tablecloth.
13. Completion of words: free—dom; green—horn.
14. Sound:[151] old—hold; guide—glide; that is, simple rhymes.
15. Faulty reactions.[152]

If we group an association experiment accordingly, we can enter these groups into a coordinate system. We then get the percentages within these fifteen groups.

The following chart is that of a family. The mother is about forty (broken line), and the girl nine years old (black line);[153] the father (dotted line) is a drunkard. The daughter produces as many word predicates as her mother. This is because mother and daughter have more than 30 percent of the associations in common; in other words, they speak an absolutely identical language in 30 percent of all cases.

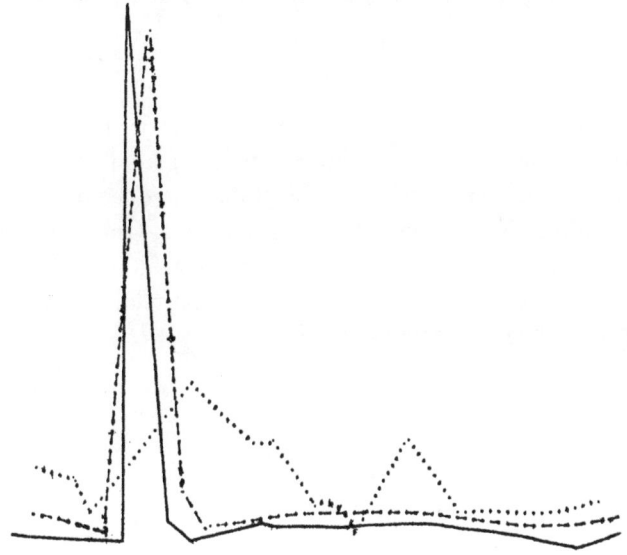

[150] In German, with its innumerable compound words, these associations would be more frequent than in English, which often uses two or more words for one German compound word.

[151] For obvious reasons, I have replaced Jung's examples by others that rhyme in English (E. F.).

[152] Kluger-Schärf: "All those associations that were none, that is, that never materialized."

[153] So in Kluger-Schärf and Hannah (p. 126). In Jung, 1909, he states, however, that the mother was forty-five and the girl sixteen.

This means that the child has become one-sidedly identical with the mother. This often occurs with women with certain marital problems. The child is identified with these and develops the attitude of a woman deeply disappointed by life, whereas she is in actual fact still a nine-year-old child! When this girl grows up, she will be ensnared in this peculiar reaction habit. Woe betide the man who comes near her! He will be entrapped in the net. Often she will turn a man immediately into an alcoholic. Consciously she chooses a teetotaler, but through a certain devilish fate the man begins to drink all the same. By way of the contrary, she leads him into the same misery. Examined in this way, however, this situation is no longer enigmatic and dark. For there is only one answer to such a woman's attitude: One must drink like a fish or otherwise be a rascal.

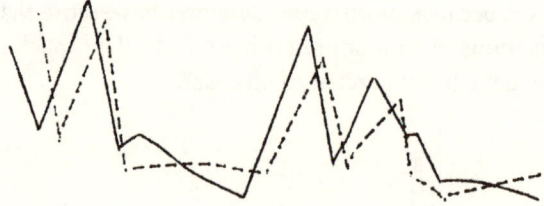

This is an example in which husband and wife are running on parallel tracks. The woman is from an utterly different kind of family, but has adjusted to her husband almost to the point where she has become identical with him. The opposite also often happens. One becomes a teetotaler, for instance, because it fits the woman's habitus. In approximately half of all marriages the man is the contained part, and the woman wears the breeches—be it openly or covertly.

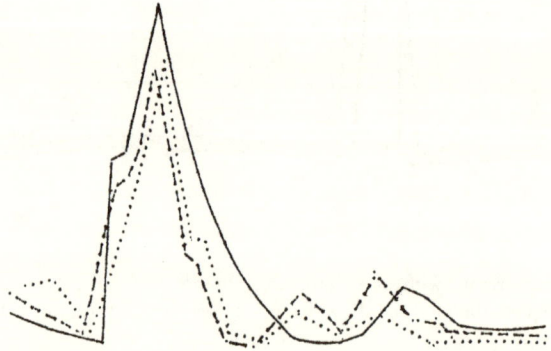

This is another case, of a man (broken line) with two daughters. He is a widower, and his daughters have adjusted themselves entirely to him.

This is naturally something that also happens; that is, it is not the wife who adjusts to the husband, but the daughter who fills this vacancy, resulting in a so-called father complex.

A calculation of averages results in the following figure:

Average difference between:	
Unrelated people	6
Related men	4.1
Related women	3.8
Fathers and children	4.2
Mothers and children	3.5
Fathers and sons	3.1
Fathers and daughters	4.9
Mothers and sons	4.7
Mothers and daughters	3
Brothers and brothers	4.7
Sisters and sisters (including married sisters)	5.1
Sisters and sisters (unmarried)	3.8
Husbands and wives	4.7

The average difference between unrelated male and female test subjects is 6. Male relatives show an average difference of 4.1; female relatives of 3.8. We see that there is less difference between the female subjects than between the male ones. This is probably accounted for by the fact that women are much more confined to the family; men already socialize at a very early age and adopt a slightly different language. It is actually quite wondrous that one can establish such differences, given that we think we speak a common language.

The difference between fathers and children is 4.2, and that between mothers and children 3.5. We see that in general children adjust more to their mothers than to their fathers, which is understandable because the womb of the family is substantially more shaped by the mother than by the father, who sits more on the edge of the nest—that is, "outside"—and flies away more often.

Now this obviously raises the question how matters stand with fathers and sons, fathers and daughters, mothers and sons, and mothers and daughters. The difference between fathers and sons is 3.1, and between fathers and daughters 4.9. That is, greater affinity exists between fathers and sons than between fathers and daughters. Gender would appear to play a role, because sons generally tend to adjust to their fathers. According to primitive superstition, the son is the reborn father. The first-born son receives[154] the soul of the father. In India, the son must inhale the dying father's last breath, because the soul leaves the body with this last breath. This is even more evident with the primitives. An old Negro had a son who would not obey him. "This fellow is standing there with my body and does not even obey me!" There are also still fathers in our part of the world who take it for granted that the son necessarily becomes like his father. It would not even occur to them that their son is somebody different from themselves. All these facts are behind the relatively close relationship between fathers and sons.

The difference between mothers and sons is 4.7, and between mothers and daughters 3.0, that is, even less than between father and children. In other words, the closest and strongest adjustment to the parental type occurs in the case of daughters in relation to their mothers. Once more, this has to do with the fact that daughters are more strongly integrated into the family; they socialize far less and they have less opportunity to leave their milieu. This is also noticeable in their speech, in that women adhere far longer to their local dialect than men. They are the actual transmitters of tradition insofar as it finds expression in language.

There is a rather great difference between brothers and sisters, namely 4.7 between brothers and 5.1 between sisters. This great difference is accounted for by the fact that married sisters are also included. If one eliminates married females, then the difference is only 3.8. The average difference between men and women is also relatively high, namely 4.7, approximately similar to the average among distant relatives, due to the fact that in many marriages such adjustment does not occur. If someone has a certain "way," this will often induce their partner to do the opposite. A wife, for instance, may love to be in fresh air, and the husband may like sitting by the fire all summer. In such cases there is a very striking difference in word reactions which puts up the average.

As the association experiment is a language experiment, certain linguistic phenomena come into consideration. I supervised a doctoral thesis that examined the components of association.[155] One finding was that in

---

[154] Rivkah Schärf: *enthält* = contains; probably a typo for *erhält* = receives.
[155] Fürst, 1907.

a series of perseverations there occurs the phenomenon of a phonetic perseveration, for instance, a sequence of vocals:

13 sharp
14 farm
15 harm
16 old fart[156]
etc.

It has become apparent that vowel sequences always occur when a complex perseverates. In other words, whenever a complex appears, it tends to elicit a phonetic series. This almost seems to be a sort of chinoiserie,[157] but is highly interesting nevertheless, because there is always a certain emotion that comes to the fore together with the complex, and this emotion then casts a spell over language. For instance, one involuntarily begins to rhyme and to use alliterations; agglutinations[158] occur. Turkish and Hungarian, for instance, are agglutinative languages, as are primitive ones that have no fixed vowels, only consonants.

When I speak of the king—and the word for king is "melek"—then I must utter the entire sentence with an "e" because the stressed main word contains an "e" as its main vowel. All subsequent words change accordingly. The main word determines the vowel character of the entire sentence. This occurs mainly in the case of primitives, because every mental process is underscored by a certain emotion. If something is not emotionally underlined, it does not enter consciousness, and so it comes to pass in the dark. This happens when primitives sit around silently and are apparently not thinking at all. What then occurs is what is called reflection or contemplation in the case of ordinary people. This process is completely unconscious in primitives, because the unemotional is completely unconscious. Thus it happens that when they make a statement, it has the characteristics of a complex. So when emotion arises, a fatal compulsion to rhyme may also arise. The language of poets, too, is also distinctly emotional and tends toward metrical form.

One more small detail: In the association experiment, complexes can be unconscious, but they can also be conscious. If the stimulus word touches upon a conscious complex, breathing becomes deeper, as if one

---

[156] The alliterations in Jung's examples in German (*scharf; Acker; schade; alt*) are not directly translatable.

[157] A decorative, or ornamental, style in Western art, especially popular in the eighteenth century, characterized by the use of Chinese motifs and techniques.

[158] In linguistics, the fusion or merging of words or word parts.

were inhaling more deeply. A different picture emerges if the stimulus has struck an unconscious complex. Then breathing is inhibited, as if the thorax muscles were contracted or inhibited, so that inspiration is somewhat inhibited until it resumes its normal character.

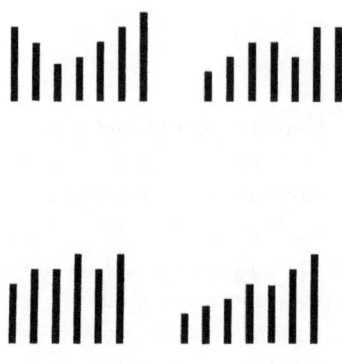

In the example on the left, a conscious complex has been touched, the breathing goes down a little, as in a sigh, and is then deepened again. In the example on the right, an unconscious complex has been touched, resulting in a real disturbance and inhibited breathing.

On the left, we see the breathing after an indifferent word, and on the right after a stimulus word that touched a complex.

The main finding is thus the insight into the existence of complexes, that is, of contents whose behavior is different from that of ordinary psychic contents, which we call factual or indifferent. Complexes are emotionally charged contents. The emotion need not be conscious; one might even say that as a rule it is unconscious. These contents also show the characteristics of a conflict, insofar as they are not smoothly woven into the web of human consciousness; they do not really belong there, but instead disturb and pierce it, and turn out to be autonomous.[159] They are foreign bodies, as it were, which cannot be ruled by the will. They have their own spontaneous character. They torment and disturb us. When a complex is touched, memory is almost invariably affected and a word vanishes, or we remember it too well and it keeps recurring. A complex always induces unconsciousness.

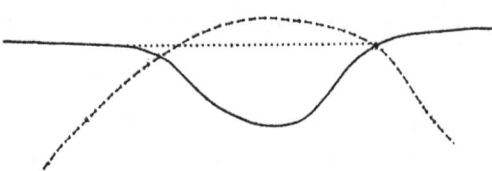

If we think of the unconscious (black line) as a straight line, this diagram shows the effect of a complex (broken line) coming up. The complex rises and takes command,

---

[159] Here the notes of Rivkah Schärf break off. Since Sidler did not take notes for this lecture (see note 149), the text for the rest of this lecture is taken over from Hannah (pp. 130–131).

and consciousness sinks as it does so. There is an *abaissement du niveau mental*.[160] When the level of consciousness sinks, there is no energy left in the will. The complex rules us; we are possessed by it. We drop from an active state into that of a passive sufferer. Ideas of ghosts arise from this process. Our very language reveals this, in such expressions as "He is beside himself" or "The devil is riding him."

Primitives understand this state very well, although primitives have no analysts and are not conscious of their complexes. They often feel alienated from themselves and then know that they have lost one of their five or six souls. These souls are not under their control, so it is very easy for one to go astray, and the primitive then performs ceremonies in order to regain it. Witch doctors are very helpful in this respect. Perhaps the primitive goes to the witch doctor and says, "Have you seen a soul flying by?" The witch doctor goes to a tree covered in bird cages, some empty with open doors and others with birds in them. He examines the cages and may say, "Yes, I have your soul bird here." Then the primitive lies down, and the witch doctor lays a trail of grains of rice from the cage to the head of the bereaved one. When the door is opened, the bird, eating grain by grain, arrives at the head where it belongs and is once more integrated. The matter is now in order. In our language, this is the integration of an unconscious content. If we were only simple and objective, we should see these things much as the primitives do. These autonomous contents are often possessed of the liveliest energy; a man beats his wife or ill-treats his children; someone else gets hysterics or a neurosis—the primitives call it all being possessed by a devil. Today we call the devils complexes, but it is a matter of indifference to the devil by what name we call him. His effect is much the same in any case. Some modern people, however, understand much better if you use primitive language and ask them to find out what is possessing them. When we are in a rage, we must be objective about it and ask ourselves what is making us so angry. A complex is a most objective thing, and the only thing we can do is to be objective about it. The cleverest intelligence cannot master a complex. A professor with an anxiety mania can classify it and perhaps banish it during the day, but right when he gets to bed out comes the complex, and he cannot sleep for terror. To say "It is only a neurosis" has no effect on it whatever, for it is

---

[160] A term coined by Jung's erstwhile teacher Pierre Janet (1859–1947). Jung's work abounds with references to Janet's notions, such as *abaissement du niveau mental, fonction du réel, dissociation, sentiment d'incomplétude, formes inférieures et supérieures* (of mental life), or *idées fixes subconscientes*, and Jung repeatedly acknowledged his debt to him.

like a bad ghost following him. If we assume that we are just egos and can, so to speak, count our chickens before they are hatched, we are likely to find out that we miscalculated. Complexes have to be taken seriously, they have dynamic energy, they live in our psyche, and they seem to be bad things; yet it is these very complexes that lead us to our fate.

Each complex has its given quantity of energy, but as it crosses the border of consciousness and takes command of us, it seizes our energy to increase its own, and our consciousness sinks down powerless and helpless. This process will persist in a family for generation after generation. The energy possessed by each complex means a reduction of the energy that is at our disposal. We may say that they are independent units and that we pay the costs of their maintenance; they rob our life of its continuity.

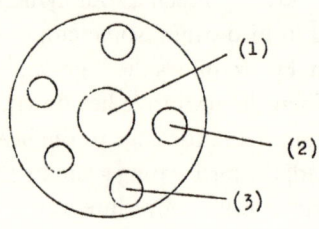

The I is also a complex. The following diagram shows it in the center (1) with other autonomous pieces (2, 3, etc.) moving about our psyche.

The question is: Have these autonomous pieces a consciousness of their own, and if so, what sort of a consciousness is it? They definitely have, but probably it is a lower consciousness than our own, an unpleasant consciousness. Complexes are so to speak our family ghosts.

Lecture 11

6 July 1934[161]

I AM VERY GLAD that a question has been asked, concerning the discussion of complexes: "Why are complexes evoked only by certain stimulus words in the first place, since from earliest childhood on we have transgressed so many interdictions issued by our parents, godparents, teachers, and so forth, to the extent that we ought to have grown a veritable felt cover of complexes, so that in actual fact every word would have to strike a complex."

There are people who are so infamous that they are able to do all kinds of things without developing a complex. Thus, a bad conscience or moral guilt does not always result in a complex. When complexes do arise, however, they condense in an economical way. If someone is particularly sensitive to this topic, he will most probably develop a moral complex, and then it will be as though he were "ridden by the devil." As a consequence, he will have to commit ever-new transgressions so that the complex will be confirmed. For the complex has the unpleasant characteristic that one forever does what tempts one, thereby inducing a kind of vicious circle. There are indeed cases in which every stimulus word hits upon a complex, but these are usually mentally ill persons. In such cases, the complex assimilates the entire association activity. You will then be able to elicit nothing in these people but precisely their complexes, for which they create a specific language. Normal persons, however, do not have this. There, complexes solidify with particular stimulus words.

There is still another reason for this. For instance, if three important complexes are present in an individual, and these are joined by a fourth, this latter complex can, due to its novelty or force, overlay the already existing ones, or push them into the background. These complexes have magnetic power; they draw things into themselves, and sometimes a very

[161] Rivkah Schärf's notes for this lecture are missing.

strong one will absorb all the weaker ones. Here, too, the law of energy applies: There is only a certain overall quantity of energy available, so that, if new complexes appear, they will devaluate all the others. This became evident at the outbreak of the World War. A large number of neurotics suddenly became able to cope with life again and enlisted in the military. In most cases, however, the neurosis returned directly after the war. Or when a life-threatening illness appears, insane or hysterical patients suddenly become reasonable again, because then they know what is hurting them and where. The moment the illness is over, however, the hysteria or mental illness reappears. In former times, one used to rub in a burning lotion on people's heads, so that they would know what was wrong with them. So long as this hurt like hell, they were perfectly reasonable.

A second question asked whether complexes can be made to disappear by taking certain provisions. So, yes, in actual fact this is the case. Complexes can disappear through atonement or a confession, either by the patient resuming a reasonable life style or through reintegration into the community. For it lies in the nature of complexes that they separate individuals from one another. Complexes are utterly inhuman things, and it is quite impossible to reach any understanding of others with their help. Just as the complex is an independent quantity per se, the person affected is thus separated from others. Complexes always make us "peculiar," and unless we pull ourselves together that's what we will be. One therefore also asks, "What's the matter with you?"[162] That is, do you possess anything hidden?

Now if someone has a strong complex, he will be possessed by it, and thus be alienated from humanity. Through the complex he will be, as it were, taken away. There is an age-old therapy for this, however: namely, confession. By way of confession, the Roman Catholic Church enables people to get away from their complexes and to return to the community. This ancient therapy is a consecration by initiation, which includes the avowal of sins. This is by no means an invention of the Catholic Church, but was one of the means of initiation before being introduced to the mysteries. On a primitive level, the matter is naturally somewhat different from what it is on a higher level, because other moral terms exist there. In ancient Egypt, the adept would speak the following words, according to a particular formula: "I have *not* done such and such!"; "I have not

---

[162] Note: *Hast du etwas?* Literally, have you got something?

deceived the wise"; or "I have not stolen people's possessions"; etc. What he actually did do, however, will not come to light in this way.

The fact that we have done away with confession in the Protestant church is one of the reasons for the compensatory movement. At least 80 percent of my patients over the last thirty years have been Protestants.[163] I have also had a good number of Jews, but only very few Catholics, because if the latter use confession rightly they do not become neurotic or separated from other people.[164] There is still another way of ridding oneself of a complex, namely by getting into some kind of continuity[165] that commits the same sin. One then no longer has a sin, but rather the feeling that one's sins are shared with a collective, and then you have at most a national complex, for instance.

* * *

As there is only one more lecture in this semester, we will now leave the subject of complexes and turn to some fundamental principles of dream psychology. The association experiment is indeed an experiment, but it is no use experimenting with dreams, because there you are dealing with the raw material provided by nature itself. Thus you are dealing with a material that is extremely delicate and unreliable. At first sight, all certainties come to an end there. With dreams, one generally assumes, "Well, something quite different could still come to mind." It is as if we had nothing but foam in our hands, and particularly so if we are expected to publicly account for what a dream in actual fact means.

The dream, like the complex, is an invasion from the unconscious. Complexes are psychic contents that all of a sudden thrust their way through our conscious contents. Dreams are incursions that somehow intrude into the dozing consciousness of the sleeper. Contrary to conscious contents, they have a peculiar character and are in no way under our control.

---

[163] In 1930, 74.2 percent of the population in the Canton of Zurich were Protestant, and 22.9 percent Roman Catholic (*Statistisches Handbuch des Kantons Zürich*, 1949, p. 30). With thanks to Ulrich Hoerni.

[164] The following passage is only in Hannah (pp. 132–133): "The Oxford Movement is a modern compensation and one which works just in as far as the right sins are confessed, but that is a hard and difficult task; there are thousands of subterfuges and alleys in which to hide. We are all willing to say 'I have not killed my neighbor, I have not done this or that' or even 'I have done this or that' but the *real sin*, the thing we did which separated us from humanity, does not come out."

[165] Maybe a hearing mistake for "collectivity."

I found it very interesting to discuss dreams with primitives when I had the opportunity. After all, you can't talk about dreams with educated people, because everybody will tell you: "I don't have any dreams, and if I do, I'll have forgotten them in the morning." So when in East Africa I tried to speak with the natives about their dreams—and though the ordinary primitive has a certain feeling for psychic things—he could say nothing about dreams, but only looked hopefully at the medicine man. When I asked the medicine man, he told me: "Well, these men do not dream; only the chief and the medicine man do. But now they only have small dreams," and tears came into his eyes. "Since the English have arrived in the country, we no longer have big dreams." It is so to speak the political or statesmanlike function of the chief to dream, and particularly to have big dreams.[166]

I am able to teach my patients and pupils early in their analysis to make the distinction between small and big dreams. Small dreams are insignificant, fragmented, and unclear dreams, which are only about personal matters, whereas big dreams are impressive, can accompany us through our entire lives, and sometimes change us through and through. These are exactly the kind of dreams that the medicine man had in mind. They always have a certain significance for the life of the tribe, and therefore must be told before the entire tribe. A palaver of all men of the tribe is called. Then the chief asks, "What is the subject of this evening's gathering?" The man who had the dream stands up and says, "As I was lying in such and such a position"—this is described in great detail—"I had such and such a vision," which he then recounts. All the people listen very attentively, think of the dream, and remain silently seated, until they are deeply impressed by the dream. Then the chief says, "Our business is done." Thereafter, everyone rises and goes home. Thus people afford themselves the time to let the dream affect them, because they are really interested in it, even if they do not understand it. The Swahilis will then discuss for hours whether a dream is favorable or unfavorable for an undertaking, and if it is voted unfavorable, the most important of Europeans will find that his expedition is being delayed because the porters will refuse to continue that

---

[166] Jung told this story various times, e.g., in 1931 [1930], § 128; or in 1962, pp. 294–295, where he added: "His reply showed me that the medicine man had lost his *raison d'être*. The divine voice which counseled the tribe was no longer needed because 'the English knew better.' Formerly the medicine man had negotiated with the gods or the power of destiny, and had advised his people. . . . Now the medicine man's authority was replaced by that of the D.[istrict] C.[ommissioner]."

day. All my Somali boys carried dream books with them and pondered their dreams every morning.

As you know, we do not share this appreciation of dreams among the primitives, at least not officially. No one dares admit to being much impressed by a dream. Our peasants laugh at the idea of their cows being bewitched, just as a councilman will not dare admit that he is superstitious. And yet they seize the first opportunity to secretly visit the Capuchin monk,[167] because they are still deeply impressed by these primeval truths. People scoff at ghosts, but in fact they are convinced of their existence. Officially, dreams are underestimated, but privately we allow them to impress us. When dealing with illness, doctors, too, are inclined to overrate the objective side, but the subjective plays a large role, especially with neurotics.

Dreams have this in common with complexes: namely, they thrust themselves forward all of a sudden. It therefore occurred to me early on that dreams are simply complexes. For instance, someone needs to make a journey, notably one that somehow gets on his nerves. Perhaps something important is at stake, or he is simply nervous about the upcoming trip. Naturally, the more complexes one has, the more complicated such simple matters become, and one may then dream of arriving late for the train, one cannot run, has lost the ticket, forgotten the wallet, and stands as though rooted to the spot and watches the train leave, and so on. So, this is a correct representation of the complex-related anxiety about the forthcoming event. Or someone who has requested an appointment with me dreams that I have notified him that it is impossible to keep our appointment at that particular time, or that there is already someone else in the consultation room when he arrives, or that the door to the consultation room is open and a lady is sitting there eavesdropping, and so forth. In the case of examinations, one derives particular pleasure from dreaming that one has failed. Women especially are liable to such dreams. If, however, you have experienced something highly impressive, you can be absolutely certain that you will *not* dream of this! Ancient wisdom thus

---

[167] Cf. Volume 1 (2018, p. 95): "So when a mountain farmer notices one day that his cow is giving less milk than usual, he immediately runs to the Capuchin monk to fetch a prayer card of Saint Anthony. The next day, the cow might in fact give again as much milk as before. The farmer, however, tells no one that he has been to see the monk; on the contrary, should anyone inquire whether he believes in demons or ghosts, he will laugh and exclaim: 'Oh no, what nonsense!' But he says this only because he is seeking election to the local council."

holds—and no, this is not my invention!—that the groom does not dream of his bride; and if he does nevertheless, something is amiss.

I once had a woman patient, a medical student and a very rational person, who was obsessed by the idea that dreams consisted entirely of previous experience. One day she arrived triumphant. The day before she had been to the dentist's and then had a dream in which everything happened "exactly as it had happened on that day." "Was everything really the same?" She then admitted to "trifling" differences—the nameplate on the door had my name on it instead of the dentist's, and the latter had of course worn a white lab coat, but it was not exactly a coat, but a nightgown! The rest can be left to the imagination.[168]

Dreams never exactly repeat an experience, they *always* have a *meaning*. They are actually like association experiments turned inside out. In these experiments, we have stimulus words that strike the complex and elicit it to emerge, whereas dreams themselves produce the test words. Dreams bring up a system of stimulus words, words that refer to the underlying meaning. If you emphasize these words and certain motifs that often recur in dreams, it is really revealing when you ask, "What comes to your mind about this?"

Dreams are chaotic territory, wondrous and changeable, but certain groups stand out clearly. First of all there are body stimulus dreams, that is, somatic stimulus dreams, which represent images of stimuli, as it were. The position of the body while sleeping may produce dreams, for instance, or a real noise can work itself into a dream in a most peculiar way. When I was a student, I was woken every morning at six. One morning I dreamt of serious diplomatic troubles between Switzerland and a foreign state. The situation became increasingly worse; in the newspapers there appeared big headlines: "Threat of war!" Crowds were gathering in the streets, troops marching past, the sound of shooting could be heard, a cannon was fired off—and then I woke up because the maid was knocking on the door.[169] From other areas, we know that it is possible for psychic contents to cross our minds almost timelessly, as if there were no time. We have very good reason to assume that in the unconscious state psychic contents are not subject to certain categories to which consciousness is subject. People drowning or falling down a mountain may re-experience

---

[168] The last phrase only in Hannah (p. 134). Jung told the same anecdote in more detail in his seminar on children's dreams (1987 [2008], pp. 22–23).

[169] In the seminar on children's dreams, Jung added: "I had the clear impression that the dream had lasted for a very long time and come to a climax with the knocking" (ibid., p. 9).

their whole lives in the second before losing consciousness. It is as if we were all of a sudden getting an overview of a huge painting with an awful lot of details. Dreams possess an incredible wealth of possibilities, with only a few images or words. If they were translated into conscious language, it would take a very long time. It is as if another time reigned in the dream, and as if something existed there that knew and saw much more than we do.

Other typical somatic dreams include indigestion dreams. For example, when we feel peristaltic movements of the intestines, we may dream of snakes. Another example: I am a good sailor, but once I too had to pay my tribute to Neptune. I was crossing from Harwich to the Hook of Holland, after I had had a very good dinner in London. It was a very stormy night, and I went straight to bed and to sleep. I dreamt of a circular staircase; a package lay at its bottom. All of a sudden, the staircase began to revolve, and the package started to ascend. *That is very practical*, I thought, but then someone turned a corkscrew against me and I thought: *They should not do that*. At the same moment, the package reached the top of the staircase. I thought, *Now someone should take it from me!* and woke up. But by then it was already too late!

When I was in the tropics suffering a fever attack, I dreamt of a Negro who was wearing a white jacket. He wanted to curl my hair with very long, red and hot curling irons. I said, "This is ridiculous! You are singeing my hair!" He replied that he wanted to make my hair curly all over, like a Negro's. Then I knew that this was my first encounter with "blackness under the skin," the first sign of "going black." It was a fever dream, but it is a real process that all Europeans who are in Africa for some time undergo.[170]

There are also dreams that are simply wish fulfillments and compensations. If you are starving or fasting, you will dream of delicious food; if you are too hot, you may dream of snow. People who have eaten too much and have heart palpitations dream that they are rushing up a mountain or are as light as feathers, and fly upward into the sky to everyone's amazement. If these dreams multiply, however, it is often a sign of heart trouble. People confined to their beds for a long time often dream of dancing or jumping, or of long hikes. During the war, soldiers in the trenches often dreamt of peaceful Sundays in the village street, and so on. If those dreams

---

[170] The last phrase is Hannah's (p. 135). See p. 4 and note 31 and the cross-reference to *MDR*, in which Jung states that this peril only threatens "the uprooted European" (1962, p. 273).

stopped, however, and people began to dream of grenades, then one knew it was time to send them back home because of an imminent "shell shock";[171] the unconscious was no longer able to remove these impressions from the dream. Like a magic carpet, the unconscious takes us where we would like to be.[172] Or you may have more or less everything that a human being needs in life—a roof over your head, a bed to sleep in, enough to eat—you need not fear being killed when you step into the street, etc. Now if someone is in such a situation and then has unpleasant dreams that torture him at night, this too is a compensation. People who do not work and squander their lives naturally have very bad dreams, because they deserve a good thrashing every night, as it were. When this function of the dream is not working, it is a danger sign.

There are also affect dreams,[173] usually when affects have failed to reach consciousness during the day, or also dreams of admonishment or dreams that inform us. A businessman, for instance, is very preoccupied with a new venture and delighted at the new opportunities. Then, at night, he dreams that he has completely dirtied his hands. And indeed it was a dirty business.

Finally, let me mention philosophical dreams, which dream for us what we failed to think during the day. We should all think a lot more. We[174] are mostly very lazy in this respect, and when we do think we usually think wrongly.

Next week we will deal with the technique of interpretation.

---

[171] This expression is in English in the notes.
[172] This formulation is Hannah's (p. 135). Sidler has: "Like with a magic cloak, the unconscious removes everything unpleasant from us."
[173] Sidler has "complex dreams."
[174] This phrase only in Hannah (p. 135).

Lecture 12

13 July 1934[175]

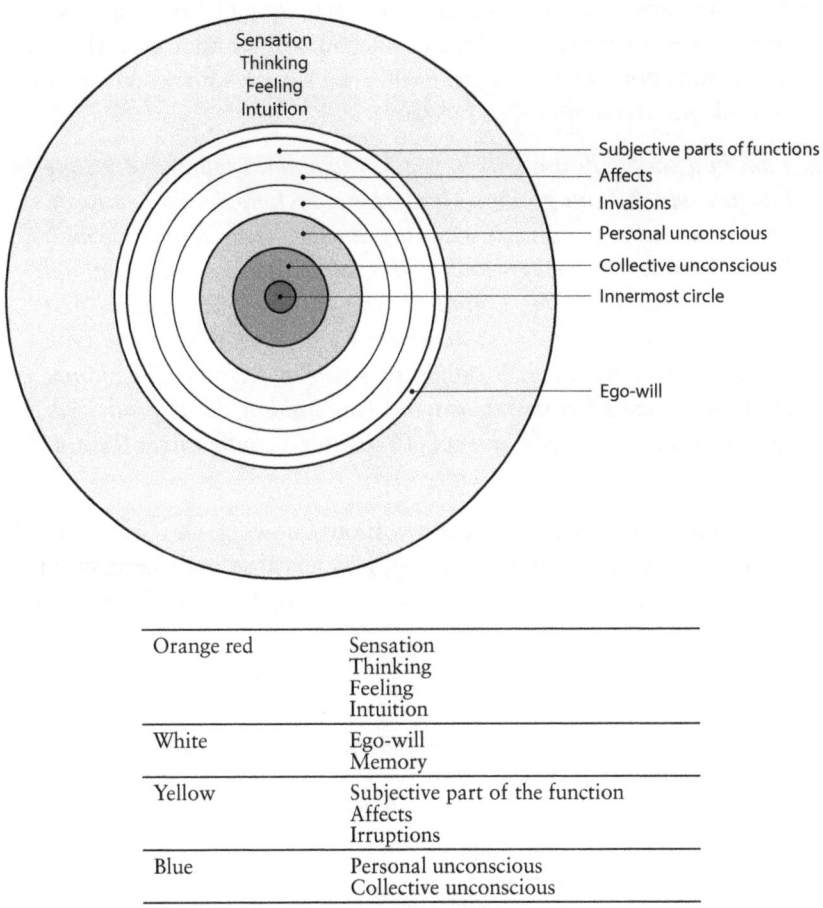

Orange red	Sensation Thinking Feeling Intuition
White	Ego-will Memory
Yellow	Subjective part of the function Affects Irruptions
Blue	Personal unconscious Collective unconscious
Shaded white	Innermost circle

---

[175] Only Sidler's notes of this lecture start with the following graph and its legend, although there seems to be no further reference to it in the lecture itself.

* * *

There are a few questions.[176] The first question is where in the literature of antiquity the legend of Ajor [sic][177] occurs. This is in Ovid's *Metamorphoses*. The quote, "..." [sic], is from a mosaic in the Cathedral of Verona.[178] I have brought along the monograph on the psychogalvanic phenomenon.[179]

* * *

In the last lecture, I gave you a general overview of various types of dreams. Today, I will give you an example of the technique of breaking down a dream.[180] It is a very simple dream, but you will see that even the simplest dream is not so very simple. I will read the dream text to you, and would ask you to commit it to memory.

> *I am in a simple house with a peasant woman. I tell her of a long journey which I am going to undertake, to Leipzig, and on foot, which astonishes her greatly. Looking outside, I see a landscape with haymakers. In the background of this landscape, a colossal animal appears all of a sudden, a kind of crab or lizard. The animal first moves toward the left, then toward the right, so that in the end I am standing in its middle as if caught in a pair of scissors. The animal approaches and I feel threatened, but I am holding a small rod, with which I hit it, and it drops dead. Thereafter I contemplate the animal for a long time and very intensely.*

We cannot interpret such a dream without knowing who dreamed it. I therefore owe you a preliminary report, which is absolutely necessary for dream analysis. The dreamer is an academic, aged about forty, a man who

---

[176] Questions and answers only in Sidler, who obviously did not catch everything.

[177] So in Sidler; possibly a typo for Amor, whose story with Psyche occupies a large part of the *Metamorphoses or the Golden Ass*, not by Ovid, but by Apuleius (ca. 124–ca. 170 CE), a work to which Jung repeatedly referred.

[178] Probably the quote Jung mentioned in the first lecture: "*In patientia vestra possidebitis animas vestras.*" See note 44.

[179] Jung published three papers on this topic (1907a; Jung & Peterson, 1907; Jung & Ricksher, 1907/08).

[180] Jung briefly mentioned the following case already in *Psychological Types* (1921, § 565), and described it and the following three dreams in more detail elsewhere (e.g., 1934 [1931], §§ 297–305; 1935 [1934], pp. 50–55; 1944, pp. 325–333; the most detailed version is in 1968 [1935], §§ 161–201).

has at last come a long way.[181] He has "suffered" great success in his particular field, but it is always a loss to have great success! He has risen to a leading position, in any event, a position that was promising in many respects; at least comparable to one who has begun an ascent at sea level in the morning and has climbed up to a height of 6,500 feet by lunchtime, reaching a high plain, from which he sees the mountains standing 13,000 feet tall, and thinking, "Well now, let's take that one in our stride too!"

There seemed to be no obstacle, and yet he developed a very peculiar neurosis, which then prompted him to consult me. He often felt strangely sick, and he suffered dizzy spells, for instance, when standing at the top of a flight of stairs, and a certain fear of falling down seized him. So he avoided elevated places from which one could look far down. He had an accelerated pulse rate and a range of other symptoms, which all together amounted to a curious clinical picture, which one also comes across elsewhere, and which is known as mountain sickness. He presented all the known symptoms: anxiety, insecurity, dizziness, even nausea, a heavy head, and difficulty in breathing. When I pointed this out, he too found it peculiar, and admitted that as a young man he had once suffered from mountain sickness with exactly the same symptoms. I asked him, "Tell me, have you perhaps had any strange dreams?" "Yes, two of them last night as a matter of fact!" Here is the first dream:

> *He comes into a small village. A few farmers are standing about. He is wearing a top hat and a handsome black suit. He is carrying a thick book under his arm and looks very dignified. He thinks: They are in for a surprise! A few boys pass by, and he recognizes his former schoolmates. He hears one of them say to the other, "He doesn't put in an appearance very often!"*

The second dream:

> *He awakens (in the dream), and knows that he must go on an important journey that day. He knows that the train is scheduled to depart at eight o'clock. It is already ten to eight. He dresses frantically, collects his documents and papers, his bag, and rushes out of the house. Suddenly he remembers that he has forgotten his portfolio at home. He rushes back, finds it eventually, dashes out of the house again, but hardly makes any progress, as if glued to the ground, and*

---

[181] He was "the director of a great public school, a very intelligent fellow" (Jung, 1968 [1935], § 161).

finally arrives at the station only to see the train departing. At first he is aghast. But then he notices a strange thing: The railway track isn't straight but is strangely S-shaped once it leaves the station, and the train is a very long one. It occurs to him that if the driver puts on full steam and rushes ahead when the engine reaches the straight part of the line the train with the carriages behind the locomotive will derail. The engine driver, what a fool, indeed accelerates fully. He shouts and waves his arms, but the engine driver doesn't hear him, and he continues to accelerate. The last carriages are thrown off the tracks, and there's a terrible accident, upon which he awakens.

So this is a typical anxiety dream.[182]

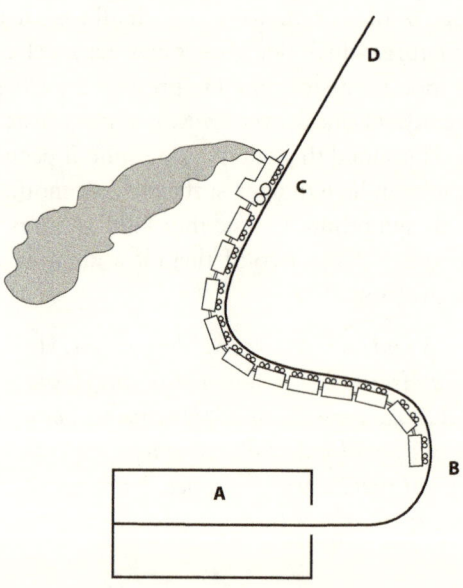

The dreamer comes from a humble background. The village in the dream is his home village. The thick book is meant to express his erudition. Indeed, he seldom returns to the village. So the first dream is a reminder of where he comes from and what he originally was. The second dream, in contrast, shows his goal and his future prospects. Despite his best and most frantic efforts, he fails to reach his objective. The engine driver is not for one moment thinking that there is a long train behind him and moves full steam ahead, as if the locomotive were on its own.

We won't fully interpret these latter two dreams as their meaning is fairly obvious, but there are a number of themes in the first dream that act like stimulus words. We will treat the dream as an association test, and take test words out of it.[183]

---

[182] Jung gave a more detailed interpretation of this man's dreams in the Tavistock Lectures (1936 [1935], §§ 161–201).

[183] This phrase only in Hannah (p. 137).

Peasant woman	We notice, for instance, that the dreamer is with a *peasant woman* in a simple house. Let's make a mental note of this.
Long journey	Then we come across the idea of a *long journey*.
Haymakers	Then there comes something like an intermezzo. While he is telling the peasant woman that he intends to take a long trip to Leipzig, all of a sudden the landscape with *haymakers* appears outside.
Monster	In this landscape, a *monster* appears all of a sudden, half crab and half lizard. Dreams often blend animals in this way.
Left-right	Then we have this strange movement of the animal, first to the right, and then to the left,[a] thus, the *right-left motif*.
Rod	Then the motif of the rod, with which he obviously kills the giant animal in a magical way.
Contemplation[b]	Finally, there is the evidently significant remark at the end that he *gazes intensely* at the animal for a long time after having killed it.

[a] Sic; in the dream text as told by Jung, and also in his following interpretative remarks, the crab-lizard moves first to the left and then to the right (also in 1968 [1935], § 180).
[b] Notes: *Betrachtung*. See note 166.

A dream should always be written down at once, otherwise we inevitably lie to ourselves. It is best to note it down on a sheet of paper that is divided into three columns: The first column is for the text; the second is for the context, that is, comments on the keyword and our associations with it, as if this were a complex word. In the third column, we can note the interpretation. This is the way to work on a dream humbly, by oneself, when there is no accomplished analyst at hand to do the work.

Text (dream motifs)	*Context (associations)*	*Interpretation*
Peasant woman	Widow	–
Simple cottage	There is a long pause, then he mentions the infirmary[a] near St. Jakob	–
Haymakers	Picture in his house	

[a] *Siechenhaus*, a hospital for incurables.

When I asked him about his associations to the "peasant woman," he said: "a widow, a woman providing lodging, a completely uneducated person." Then there was a long pause, for it was most unpleasant for him to remember that his mother was a poor widow. He had been so successful, and had traveled so far from his humble origins, that he greatly preferred indulging vague fantasies of a possible noble origin instead of remembering the fact that he came from such a humble background. Here we have the so-called motif of the two mothers. Heroes and pharaohs have always entertained the notion that they have two different pairs of parents, human and divine ones. On the outer walls of the pyramids, the actual story is depicted, while inside, in the "birth chamber," there is a depiction of two Gods copulating. We find the same motif in the heroes of Greek mythology, even if it was only the milk that was divine, as in the case of Heracles: "She wrested her breast from his mouth, and the milk spurted over the heavens and formed the Milky Way."[184] This motif of the double origin lies in the collective unconscious.

So it is quite inconvenient for him to remember his humble origins. With regard to the "simple house," at first he says that nothing occurs to him. In such cases, patients proceed a bit further, and then after some time bring some far-fetched association. Thus, all of a sudden he recalls the infirmary near St. Jakob an der Birs, where 1,500 brave Swiss lost their lives in 1444.[185] In such cases we must remember that it was the patient himself who gave this seemingly absurd association, and it was not as stupid as it appeared, for he himself was contemplating a slaughter, not of 1,500 Swiss indeed, but of one poor monster.[186] Except that he is taking the easy way out by doing it with a magic rod.

---

[184] According to Greek/Roman mythology, Hera/Juno was tricked by her husband Zeus/Jupiter into breast feeding his illicit son Heracles/Hercules as a baby while she was asleep, in order to give Heracles immortality. When Hera awoke and realized who he was, she immediately tore him from her breast, and her milk squirted across the sky to form the Milky Way.

[185] In the legendary battle of St. Jakob an der Birs, on 26 August 1444, 1,500 Swiss fought against a French mercenary army of about 20,000–30,000 men just outside the city walls of Basel. Except for some fifteen soldiers who could get away, the Swiss army were eventually killed to the last man, the last of them in the small hospital of St. Jakob, to which they had retreated. The French troops suffered such heavy losses, however, that they turned back, and eventually a peace treaty was signed between France and the Swiss Confederacy and Basel. The battle became a symbol of Swiss military bravery in the face of overwhelming odds, finding explicit mention in the Swiss national anthem (until 1961).

[186] Thus in Hannah (p. 138). Sidler: ". . . for he himself was about to die a heroic death, like the 1,500 Swiss."

The journey to Leipzig replicates a fantasy. He had studied in Leipzig, and his ambition was not satisfied with the university at which he already held a leading position. He wishes to be offered a chair at the University of Leipzig; the university impressed him at the time, so he believes he would be in at least seventh heaven if he made it there. So he shares his ambition with this simple woman who is tremendously astonished at this project. Then the haymakers appear. He associates a picture of haymakers on the wall of his house. This leads him back to his childhood, when he had helped the haymakers, which would have been a far simpler association, but which he does not like to remember because of its unpleasant background; he didn't help out because he liked it so much, but because he had to.

Up to this point, the dream is quite banal, but then it becomes creative. The unpleasant background becomes even more unpleasant with the appearance of the "regress-lizard."[187] The dream creates a monster, a non-existing animal, part lizard and part crab—which, as is well known, walks backward—though in this case it moves forward. At first, I did not press him about this monster; I only wanted to know how much of this motif he was conscious of.

Regarding the "right-left" motif, he mentioned that the left side was the unfavorable one, because the Latin word for left, *sinister*, means dark, gloomy, somber; and bad omens come from the left. Then the monster went to the right, however, and to this he had no associations. He just remarked, "When the animal moved to the right, it went to its death." The left side is always meant from the perspective of our body. It is the side of the heart. The left side is the semi-conscious, emotional side, where things happen to us as it were accidentally. The right side, on the other hand, is the purposeful, acting side, and controlled by the head. What we do on the right side is therefore "right," it is "directed." Very often "the right hand knoweth not what the left hand doeth,"[188] and very often the left side does something which the right one would prefer not to know about. This would appear to be true in the case of the dreamer. The animal first moves toward the left, signifying that the dreamer is threatened by the unconscious; then, however, he is also threatened from the right side, from consciousness. The latter he feels to be dangerous, for he does not want it in consciousness. So here matters become dangerous for the animal, for now he takes hold of the divining rod.

[187] Notes: *Regress-Eidechse*.
[188] Matthew 6, 3.

The divining rod immediately evokes a "magic wand" in his mind. This victory, however, does not make him particularly happy, for at the end he ponders it for a long time. "What were you thinking about?" "I actually don't know!" The word *betrachten*[189] is conspicuous. This good old German term seeks to express a curious action, a kind of magical action. If we *betrachten* something, we look at it intensely and for a long time. According to ancient understanding, the act of seeing involves the emission of a fluid or aura.[190] If we behold a lion or snake in the jungle for a long time, for instance, and remain still enough, then "the wiser head backs down,"[191] and the lion or the snake goes away. It is possible to bewitch people in the same way.[192] If we desire something strongly enough and look at it long enough, it will come to us. This is already known to children; when they enter their neighbor's kitchen and eye the jam for long enough, it will come to them. The same happened to the ancient Greeks: If they beheld the image of a God long enough, it would eventually blink or shake its head. If we look at and *betrachten* something long enough, it will be vitalized by our life, it will as it were be impregnated or become pregnant.[193]

I remember that as a child I used to go and visit an aunt on Sundays. There was a copper engraving of a parson on a staircase. I would keep looking at the picture until the parson moved and walked down the

---

[189] *betrachten*: to view, consider, regard, look at, behold, gaze at, contemplate, examine, observe.

[190] Plato thought of vision as a kind of touch: "And of the organs they [the Gods] constructed first light-bearing eyes, and these they fixed in the face for the reason following. They contrived that all such fire as had the property not of burning but of giving a mild light should form a body akin to the light of every day. For they caused the pure fire within us, which is akin to that of day, to flow through the eyes in a smooth and dense stream; and they compressed the whole substance, and especially the center, of the eyes, so that they occluded all other fire that was coarser and allowed only this pure kind of fire to filter through. So whenever the stream of vision is surrounded by midday light, it flows out like unto like, and coalescing therewith it forms one kindred substance along the path of the eyes' vision, wheresoever the fire which streams from within collides with an obstructing object without. And this substance, having all become similar in its properties because of its similar nature, distributes the motions of every object it touches, or whereby it is touched, throughout all the body even unto the Soul, and brings about that sensation which we now term 'seeing'" (*Timaeus*, ca. 360 BCE [1925], 45b–46c).

[191] *Der Klügere gibt nach*, German saying for which there is no exact equivalent in English.

[192] This phrase only in Hannah (p. 138).

[193] Notes: . . . *wird es mit unserem Leben erfüllt—es wird sozusagen geschwängert oder "trächtig."*

stairs.[194] Then I would be satisfied and could make my way home. This art of observation was practiced until the late Middle Ages. For many years I regarded this incident as childish, but primitives do exactly the same thing; they know the magic effect of the eye. It seems that our life can stream out of our eyes and enter the object, which will then move toward us. By contemplating and beholding this monster for such a long time, the dreamer actually attempts to make it move and bring it to life again, although he was not aware of this. For one does not kill such a monster with a divining rod. That would be far too simple! The dream gives us his whole life, and I could give you many more examples of even simpler dreams, which all share an essential characteristic—that they contain the dreamer's whole life and situation.

Let us now attempt to interpret this dream on the basis of what we know. As with a piece of drama, we call the beginning of the dream the exposition. It presents the situation in which the dreamer himself and the dream problem are situated. It is as if someone were to begin a speech by telling the sleeper: "Your problem begins in a simple house, where there is this simple woman, just like your mother. You tell her about your magnificent plans. She is impressed and amazed, but you are in fact still in this simple house; you are still a small boy living with his mother."

In every human life there exist stages, and we cannot simply leapfrog one of these. There is a certain differentiation, which forms a stage. It is by no means irrelevant at which stage or on which level someone is born. A dweller on sea level can mount perhaps 6,500 feet without suffering mountain sickness, and one who began at 6,500 feet might mount to 13,000, but the height at which we were born accompanies us through life and can never be denied. Certain boundaries are set in this respect. We cannot deny the influences that have occurred in our childhood and youth; they accompany us through our whole life. We will always be confronted with our past. It follows after us like the train carriages, or goes ahead like the engine that pulls us. Our past need not be only a dead weight; it can also be a powerful drive. The great difference between the present situation [and childhood] might represent a life motif. Bourget deals with this theme in *L'Étape*, a book which I recommend to you.[195]

---

[194] Jung told this anecdote also in the "Tavistock Lectures" (1936 [1935], § 397). The picture was of his grandfather.

[195] See note 64. The novel *L'Étape* (1902) is a study of the inability of a family rising rapidly from the peasant class to adapt itself to the new conditions.

This man has secured a considerable position for himself by the side of the hill. There is already a vast difference between where this man stands today and where he started, and he should have been satisfied. But he is rationalistic. He thinks: If he has already come such a long way in such a short time, why should he not make it even much further? He is no longer very young; he is forty. By that age we should have reached our place in life, and if someone has not, if he has still to ascend, one can only say that he is a great exception. As you know, there is a well-known biography where it says: "Up until the age of forty, he showed no signs of bearing the imprint of genius. And none afterward either!"[196]

Our dreamer is in the second half of life after reaching the meridian height,[197] after passing the stepping stone of thirty-five years. He ignored this, however, and at thirty-six a certain nervousness became apparent. One half of him wanted to press on, and the other half said, "No!" In actual fact, he is still in his childhood, and still a little boy. The exposition of the dream indicates that he should remember that he had worked with haymakers, and that his mother is a simple peasant woman. Out of this impression a frightening thought arises, of an animal that walks backward, a crab or a lizard. Both animals are cold-blooded creatures; they are not warm and are not passionate; they are cool-water animals. There is no burning desire for new ventures, no hot-blooded passion, but these are cold-blooded and even backward-moving animals that show him the way. Mythologically, this crab-lizard belongs to the category of "helpful animals," which show humans the way in critical situations, or bring them something they lack. Among the numerous other motifs in the collective unconscious—the ford, the dragon, the fairy prince, etc.—the helpful animal frequently turns up, such as the raven which brings food to the prisoner, or the wolf that suckled Romulus and Remus.[198]

The crab thought leads backward. It comes first from the unfavorable left, and then from the right, from where it threatens to become conscious. This consciousness that this animal represents the peripeteia of his life has to be prevented, and so it is killed by the dreamer with his magic wand. This wand is a magical instrument that humans possess. When we have a magic wand, we take it in our right hand; that is, we think something away. If we think it away properly, it will no longer exist. If something doesn't suit us, we will invent a rationale. The intellect is a magic wand

---

[196] Source not identified.
[197] Sidler has: "he had missed reaching the meridian height."
[198] As in the well-known legend about the founding of Rome.

with which you can prove and disprove anything, especially unpleasant things, as in this instance: "But this animal doesn't exist! It is just a dream figure." The animal is then completely done for. But what happened to the animal? Where is it really? This the dreamer does not know, and that is why he *betrachtet* it for such a long time. What has happened, however, escapes us. He cannot afford to kill this animal, since it is his natural instinct. He has lost this natural instinct, however, and he no longer recognizes it in the image of the animal, because he is rationalistic and believes in continuous progress. It is so long since this man followed his instinct that he simply does not recognize it in this monstrous form. He believed that his life was to consist of continual progress, and he is not willing to sacrifice this idea. This is the delusion of our age, to believe that there is continual progress, but continuous regression also exists! This interpretation did not enlighten the dreamer. He learned nothing from it and refused to accept my explanation of this dream. So, unfortunately, he went on following his ambitions and a disastrous situation followed. And thus it happened that after a while his comfortable seat on the mountainside also went to the devil.

Bibliography

Adler, Gerhard (1934). *Entdeckung der Seele. Von Sigmund Freud und Alfred Adler zu C. G. Jung*. Mit einem Geleitwort von C. G. Jung. Zurich: Rascher.
Bally, Gustav (1934). "Deutschstämmige Therapie." *Neue Zürcher Zeitung* (no. 343, 27 February 1934).
Baynes Jansen, Diana (2003). *Jung's Apprentice. A Biography of Helton Godwin Baynes*. Einsiedeln: Daimon.
Bergson, Henri (1907). *Creative Evolution*. Trans. Arthur Mitchell. New York: Henry Holt and Co., 1911. Reprint using original plates: Mineola, NY: Dover Publications, 1998.
Bleuler, Eugen (1912). "Zur Theorie der Sekundärempfindungen." *Zeitschrift für Psychologie*, 65: 1–39.
Boas, Franz (1912). "Changes in bodily form of descendants of immigrants." In idem, *Race, Language and Culture*, 60–77. New York: Macmillan, 1940.
Bourget, Paul (1902). *L'Étape*. Paris: Éditions Plon-Nourrit.
Condillac, Étienne Bonnot de (1754). *Traité des sensations*. 2 volumes. London, Paris: de Bure. *Traité des sensations*. In *Oeuvres de Condillac*. Revues, corrigées par l'Auteur, imprimées sur ses manuscrits autographes, et augmentées de "La Langue des Calculs," ouvrage posthume. Volume 3. Paris: Ch. Houel, 1798.
Descartes, René (1637). *Discours de la méthode pour bien conduire sa raison et chercher la verité dans les sciences*. Leyden: Jan Maire.
Falzeder, Ernst (2012). "Freud and Jung, Freudians and Jungians." *Jung Journal, Culture & Psyche* 6(3): 24–43.
Falzeder, Ernst (2016). "Types of truth: Jung's philosophical roots." *Jung Journal, Culture & Psyche*, 10(3): 14–30.
Freud, Sigmund (1910). "The antithetical meaning of primal words." In *The Standard Edition of the Complete Psychological Works of Sigmund Freud*. London: The Hogarth Press and The Institute of Psycho-Analysis, 1953–1974 [= SE], Volume 11, pp. 155–161.
Freud, Sigmund (1916–1917). *Introductory Lectures on Psycho-Analysis*. SE 15 and 16.
Freud, Sigmund (1933). *New Introductory Lectures on Psycho-Analysis*. SE 22, pp. 5–182.
Freud, Sigmund, and Max Eitingon (2004). *Briefwechsel 1906–1939*. 2 volumes. Ed. Michael Schröter. Tübingen: Edition diskord.
Freud, Sigmund, and Carl Gustav Jung (1974). *The Freud/Jung Letters: The Correspondence between Sigmund Freud and C. G. Jung*. Ed. William McGuire. Trans. Ralph Manheim and R. F. C. Hull. Cambridge, MA: Harvard University Press, corrected edition, 1988.

Frobenius, Leo (1904). *Das Zeitalter des Sonnengottes* [*The Era of The Sun God*]. Berlin: Georg Reimer.

Fürst, Emma (1907). *Statistische Untersuchungen über Wortassoziationen und über familiäre Übereinstimmung im Reaktionstypus bei Ungebildeten.* Dissertation, University of Zurich. *Journal für Psychologie und Neurologie,* 9. Also in *Diagnostische Assoziationsstudien,* Volume 2. Leipzig: Barth, 1909, pp. 77–112.

Gagliardi, Ernst (1938). "Die Universität Zürich 1833–1933." In idem et al. (eds.), *Die Universität Zürich 1833–1933 und ihre Vorläufer.* Zurich: Erziehungsdirektion, 1938.

Goethe, Johann Wolfgang von (1808–1831). *Aus meinem Leben. Dichtung und Wahrheit.* Tubingen: J. G. Cotta'ische Buchhandlung. *Hamburger Ausgabe,* Band 9, *Autobiographische Schriften I.* Munich: C. H. Beck, 12., durchgesehene Auflage 1994. *Truth and Poetry: From My Life.* Trans. John Oxenford. London: Henry G. Bohn, 1848. *From My Life: Poetry and Truth. The Collected Works,* Volumes 4 and 5. Princeton, NJ: Princeton University Press, 1994.

Grimm, Jacob, and Wilhelm Grimm (1854–1960). *Deutsches Wörterbuch.* 16 volumes. Leipzig: Hirzel. Reprint in 33 volumes: Munich: Deutscher Taschenbuch Verlag, 1984.

Hannah, Barbara (1959). *Modern Psychology.* Volumes 1 and 2: *Notes on the Lectures given at the Eidgenössische Technische Hochschule, Zürich, by Prof. Dr. C. G. Jung, October 1933–July 1935.* Second edition. Zurich: privately printed.

Hannah, Barbara (1976). *Jung, His Life and Work: A Biographical Memoir.* Boston: Shambhala, 1991.

Hinkle, Beatrice Moses (1923). *The Re-Creating of the Individual: A Study of Psychological Types and Their Relation to Psychoanalysis.* London: George Allen & Unwin.

Jaffé, Aniela (1968). *Aus Leben und Werkstatt von C. G. Jung. Parapsychologie, Alchemie, Nationalsozialismus, Erinnerungen aus den letzten Jahren.* Zurich: Rascher.

Jones, Ernest (1955). *The Life and Work of Sigmund Freud.* Volume 2: *Years of Maturity, 1901–1919.* New York: Basic Books.

Joyce, James (1922). *Ulysses.* London: Egoist Press.

Jung, C. G. (1902). *On the Psychology and Pathology of So-Called Occult Phenomena.* CW 1, pp. 3–88.

Jung, C. G. (1905a). "On the psychological diagnosis of facts." CW 1, pp. 219–221.

Jung, C. G. (1905b). "The psychological diagnosis of evidence." CW 2, pp. 318–352.

Jung, C. G. (1905c). "The reaction-time ratio in the association experiment." CW 2, pp. 221–271.

Jung, C. G. (1907a). "On the psychophysical relations of the association experiment." CW 2, pp. 483–491.

Jung, C. G. (1907b). "Association d'idées familiales." *Archives de psychologie,* 7(26): 160–168. (Not in CW.)

Jung, C. G. (1908). "New aspects of criminal psychology." CW 2, pp. 586–596.

Jung, C. G. (1909). "The family constellation." *CW* 2, pp. 466–479.
Jung, C. G. (1910 [1909]). "The association method." *CW* 2, pp. 439–465.
Jung, C. G. (1911/12). *Wandlungen und Symbole der Libido. Jahrbuch für psychoanalytische und psychopathologische Forschungen*, 1911, 3(1): 120–227; 1912, 4(1): 162–464. In book form: Leipzig: Deuticke, 1912. Reprint: Munich: Deutscher Taschenbuch Verlag, 1991. *Psychology of the Unconscious: A Study of the Transformations and Symbolisms of the Libido.* Trans. Beatrice Hinkle. New York: Moffat, Yard and Co., 1916. In revised form (1950) and under new title, *Symbole der Wandlung*, in *GW* 5; *Symbols of Transformation*, in *CW* 5.
Jung, C. G. (1913). "General aspects of psychoanalysis." *CW* 4, pp. 229–242.
Jung, C. G. (1917). *Collected Papers on Analytical Psychology*. Ed. Constance Long. London: Ballière, Tindall & Cox.
Jung, C. G. (1918). "The role of the unconscious." *CW* 10, pp. 3–28.
Jung, C. G. (1921). *Psychological Types. CW* 6.
Jung, C. G. (1928 [1931]). "A psychological theory of types." *CW* 6, pp. 524–541.
Jung, C. G. (1930a). "Psychology and literature." *CW* 15, pp. 84–108.
Jung, C. G. (1930b). "The complications of American psychology." *CW* 10, pp. 502–514.
Jung, C. G. (1931 [1927]). "Mind and earth." *CW* 10, pp. 29–49.
Jung, C. G. (1931 [1930]). "Archaic man." *CW* 10, pp. 50–73.
Jung, C. G. (1931). *Seelenprobleme der Gegenwart*. Zurich: Rascher.
Jung, C. G. (1932). "'Ulysses': A monologue." *CW* 15, pp. 109–134.
Jung, C. G. (1933a). "Zur Empirie des Individuationsprozesses." In *Eranos-Jahrbuch 1934*. Zurich: Rhein-Verlag. Revised and enlarged version, "A study in the process of individuation," in *CW* 9/1, pp. 290–354.
Jung, C. G. (1933b). "The meaning of psychology for modern man." *CW* 10, pp. 134–156.
Jung, C. G. (1934 [1931]). "The practical use of dream analysis." *CW* 16, pp. 139–161.
Jung, C. G. (1934 [1933]). "Foreword to Adler: *Entdeckung der Seele*." *CW* 18, p. 517.
Jung, C. G. (1934a). "The state of psychotherapy today." *CW* 10, pp. 157–173.
Jung, C. G. (1934b). "A review of the complex theory." *CW* 8, pp. 92–104.
Jung, C. G. (1934c). "The soul and death." *CW* 8, pp. 404–415.
Jung, C. G. (1934d). "Archetypes of the collective unconscious." *CW* 9/1, pp. 3–41.
Jung, C. G. (1934e). "Letter to *Neue Zürcher Zeitung*, 15 March 1934." *CW* 10, § 1034, fn. p. 544.
Jung, C. G. (1935 [1934]). *Bericht über das Basler Seminar*. 1–6 October 1934. Basel: privately multigraphed, 1935.
Jung, C. G. (1935). "Psychological commentary on 'The Tibetan Book of the Dead.'" *CW* 11, pp. 509–526.
Jung, C. G. (1936 [1935]). *The Tavistock Lectures: On the Theory and Practice of Analytical Psychology. CW* 18, pp. 5–182.
Jung, C. G. (1937 [1934]). "On the psychological diagnosis of evidence. The evidence-experiment in the Näf trial." *CW* 2, pp. 605–614.

Jung, C. G. (1938). "Foreword to the second German edition" [of the "Commentary on 'The Secret of the Golden Flower'"]. *CW* 13, pp. 3–5.
Jung, C. G. (1943). "The gifted child." *CW* 17, pp. 135–145.
Jung, C. G. (1944). *L'homme à la découverte de son âme*. Geneva, Annemasse: Éditions du Mont-Blanc. (Contains notes of the Basel seminar, 1935 [1934], in French translation.)
Jung, C. G. (1948). "Address on the occasion of the founding of the C. G. Jung Institute, Zurich, 24 April 1948." *CW* 18, pp. 471–476.
Jung, C. G. (1952 [1949]). "Foreword to Adler: *Studies in Analytical Psychology*." *CW* 18, pp. 523–524.
Jung, C. G. (1957). *The Undiscovered Self (Present and Future)*. CW 10, pp. 245–305.
Jung, C. G. (1958). "Schizophrenia." *CW* 3, pp. 256–272.
Jung, C. G. (1962). *Memories, Dreams, Reflections*. Recorded and edited by Aniela Jaffé. Trans. Richard and Clara Winston. London: Fontana Press, 1995.
Jung, C. G. (1968 [1935]). *Analytical Psychology, Its Theory and Practice*. The Tavistock Lectures. London: Routledge & Kegan Paul.
Jung, C. G. (1972). *Briefe I, 1906–1945*. Ed. Aniela Jaffé, in collaboration with Gerhard Adler. Olten: Walter.
Jung, C. G. (1973). *Briefe III, 1956–1961*. Ed. Aniela Jaffé, in collaboration with Gerhard Adler. Olten: Walter.
Jung, C. G. (1976). *Letters. Volume 2, 1951–1961*. Ed. Gerhard Adler, in collaboration with Aniela Jaffé. Trans. R. F. C. Hull. Hove: Routledge & Kegan Paul.
Jung, C. G. (1977). *Visions: Notes of the Seminar Given in 1930–1934*. Ed. Claire Douglas. Princeton, NJ: Princeton University Press.
Jung, C. G. (1987 [2008]). *Children's Dreams: Notes from the Seminar Given in 1936–1940*. Philemon Series. Ed. Lorenz Jung and Maria Meyer-Grass. Trans. Ernst Falzeder. Princeton, NJ: Princeton University Press, 2008.
Jung, C. G. (1988). *Nietzsche's Zarathustra: Notes of the Seminar Given in 1934–1939*. 2 volumes. Ed. James L. Jarrett. Princeton, NJ: Princeton University Press.
Jung, C. G. (1996). *The Psychology of Kundalini Yoga: Notes of the Seminar Given in 1932 by C. G. Jung*. Bollingen Series. Ed. Sonu Shamdasani. Princeton, NJ: Princeton University Press.
Jung, C. G. (1997). *Visions: Notes of the Seminar Given in 1930–1934*. 2 volumes. Ed. Claire Douglas. Princeton, NJ: Princeton University Press.
Jung, C. G. (2009). *The Red Book. Liber Novus*. Ed. Sonu Shamdasani. Trans. Mark Kyburz, John Peck, and Sonu Shamdasani. New York: W. W. Norton.
Jung, C. G. (2014). *Dream Interpretation Ancient and Modern: Notes from the Seminar Given in 1936–1941*. Philemon Series. Ed. John Peck, Lorenz Jung, and Maria Meyer-Grass. Trans. Ernst Falzeder. Princeton, NJ: Princeton University Press.
Jung, C. G. (2018). *History of Modern Psychology: Lectures Delivered at ETH Zurich. Volume 1: 1933–1934*. Philemon Series. Ed. Ernst Falzeder. Trans. Mark Kyburz, John Peck, and Ernst Falzeder. Princeton, NJ: Princeton University Press.

Jung, C. G. (forthcoming). *Modern Psychology and Dreams: Lectures Delivered at ETH Zurich*. Volume 3: *1934–1935*. Philemon Series. Ed. and trans. Ernst Falzeder. Princeton, NJ: Princeton University Press.

Jung, C. G. (in preparation [1933]). *On Dream Interpretation, Yoga and Psychology: Notes of the Seminar Given by Dr. C. G. Jung in Berlin between 26 June and 1 July 1933, with a Presentation by Heinrich Zimmer*. Philemon Series. Ed. Giovanni Sorge. Trans. Mark Kyburz and John Peck. Princeton, NJ: Princeton University Press.

Jung, C. G., et al. (1934). *Wirklichkeit der Seele. Anwendungen und Fortschritte der neueren Psychologie*. Zurich: Rascher.

Jung, C. G., and Erich Neumann (2015). *Analytical Psychology in Exile: The Correspondence of C. G. Jung and Erich Neumann*. Philemon Series. Ed. Martin Liebscher. Trans. Heather McCartney. Princeton, NJ: Princeton University Press.

Jung, C. G., and Frederick Peterson (1907). "Psychophysical investigations with the galvanometer and pneumograph in normal and insane individuals." *CW* 2, pp. 492–553.

Jung, C. G., and Charles Ricksher (1907/08). "Further investigations on the galvanic phenomenon and respiration in normal and insane individuals." *CW* 2, pp. 554–580.

Jung, C. G., and Franz Riklin (1904/05). "The associations of normal subjects." *CW* 2, pp. 3–196.

Jung, C. G., and Hans Schmid-Guisan (2013). *The Question of Psychological Types: The Correspondence of C. G. Jung and Hans Schmid-Guisan, 1915–1916*. Philemon Series. Ed. John Beebe and Ernst Falzeder. Trans. Ernst Falzeder, with the collaboration of Tony Woolfson. Princeton, NJ: Princeton University Press.

Kirsch, Thomas B. (2000). *The Jungians: A Comparative and Historical Perspective*. London: Routledge.

Kranefeldt, Wolfgang M. (1930). *Die Psychoanalyse. Psychoanalytische Psychologie*. Mit einer Einführung von C. G. Jung. Berlin: W. de Gruyter, Sammlung Göschen Nr. 1034.

Lang, Helen S. (2005). "Perpetuity, eternity, and time in Proclus' cosmos." *Phronesis*, 50(2): 150–169.

Laplanche, Jean, and Jean-Bertrand Pontalis (1967). *The Language of Psycho-Analysis*. Trans. Donald Nicholson-Smith. New York: W. W. Norton, 1973.

Lossky, Nikolay O. (1906). *The Intuitive Basis of Knowledge. An Epistemological Inquiry*. Trans. Nathalie A. Duddington. London: Macmillan & Co., 1919.

McGuire, William, and R. F. C. Hull (eds.) (1977). *Jung Speaking: Interviews and Encounters*. Bollingen Series. Princeton, NJ: Princeton University Press.

Murchison, Carl (ed.) (1925). *Psychologies of 1925*. Worcester, MA: Clark University Press.

Murchison, Carl (ed.) (1930). *Psychologies of 1930*. Worcester, MA: Clark University Press.

Naef, Max (1897). "Ein Fall von temporärer, totaler, theilweise retrograder Amnesie." *Zeitschrift für Hypnotismus* 6: 321–354.

Nietzsche, Friedrich (1886). *Jenseits von Gut und Böse*. In *Kritische Studienausgabe*, Volume 5. Eds. Giorgio Colli and Mazzino Montinari. Munich: Deutscher

Taschenbuch Verlag, revised edition, 1999. *Beyond Good and Evil.* Eds. Rolf-Peter Horstmann and Judith Norman. Cambridge: Cambridge University Press, 2002.

Pfister, Oskar (1912). "Die Ursache der Farbenbegleitung bei akustischen Wahrnehmungen und das Wesen anderer Synästhesien" [The cause of chromosthesias associated with acoustic impressions and the meaning of other synaesthesias]. *Imago, Zeitschrift für Anwendung der Psychoanalyse auf die Geisteswissenschaften* 1: 265–275.

Plato (ca. 360 BCE). *Plato in Twelve Volumes.* Volume 9. Trans. W. R. M. Lamb. Cambridge, MA: Harvard University Press/London: William Heinemann, 1925.

Roudinesco, Elisabeth, and Michel Plon (2006). *Dictionnaire de la psychanalyse. Troisième édition.* Paris: Fayard.

Semon, Richard (1921). *Mneme.* Trans. Louis Simon. London: George Allen & Unwin.

Shamdasani, Sonu (2003). *Jung and the Making of Modern Psychology: The Dream of a Science.* Cambridge: Cambridge University Press.

Shamdasani, Sonu (2005). *Jung Stripped Bare by His Biographers, Even.* London: Karnac.

Skues, Richard (2012). "Clark revisited: Reappraising Freud in America." In John Burnham (ed.), *After Freud Left. A Century of Psychoanalysis in America.* Chicago: University of Chicago Press, pp. 49–84.

Spinoza, Baruch (de) (1677). *Ethica, ordina geometrico demonstrata.* In *Spinoza Opera*, Volume 2. Ed. Carl Gebhardt. Heidelberg: Carl Winter, 1925. *Ethics.* Trans. Edwin Curley. New York etc.: Penguin Classics, 2005.

Statistisches Handbuch des Kantons Zürich (1949). Ed. Statistisches Bureau des Kantons Zürich. Zurich: Buchdruckerei Berichthaus.

Stiftung C. G. Jung Küsnacht (ed.) (2009). *The House of C. G. Jung. The History and Restoration of the Residence of Emma and Carl Gustav Jung-Rauschenbach.* Zurich: Kommissionsverlag FO-Print & Media AG.

Talbot, P. Aumary (1912). *In the Shadow of the Bush.* New York: George H. Doran Company / London: William Heinemann.

Vandercook, John W. (1925). "White magic and black: The jungle science of Dutch Guiana." *Harper's Monthly Magazine*, October 1925: 548–554. In idem, *Tom-Tom.* New York: Harper & Brothers, 1926, pp. 190–221.

Van der Hoop, Johannes Hermanus (1923). *Character and the Unconscious: A Critical Exposition of the Psychology of Freud and of Jung.* Trans. Elizabeth Trevelyan. London: K. Paul, Trench, Trubner & Co./New York: Harcourt, Brace & Co.

Wells, Herbert George (1895). *The Time Machine: An Invention.* London: Heinemann/New York: Henry Holt & Co.

Index

Page numbers in *italics* indicate figures and tables.

abaissement du niveau mental, 81, 81n160
Abernethian Society, *xxxviii*
Adler, Alfred, *xxxix*, *xlix*; individual psychology, *li*
Adler, Gerhard, *xxxii*, 25n68; *Die Entdeckung der Seele* (*The Discovery of the Soul*), *liii*n21, 25
affect: James-Lange theory of, 40; term, 39
Africa, country of Gods, 52, 52n123
agglutinations, 79
Ahnung, intuition, 19, 20
Aiolos, legend of, 8–9
Albrecht (King), 50n117; Parricida's murder of, 50
alliterations, 79
Americans, detection of, 3–4
Analytical Psychology Club, *xxxix*, *xxxv*
anima, 65, 66
animus, 65
Anti-Comintern Pact, *xxxviii*
archetypes: ford crossing, 52; term, 50
association(s): internal and external types of, 70–71n146; method of collective unconscious, 55–56
association experiments, 55–56, 57; conscious and unconscious complexes, 79–81; discovery of complexes, 70; dream psychology, 85–90; elderly gentleman example, 57–58; emotional states, 66; family, 75–78; Jung and Fürst, 74n149; language, 78–79; neurotic person example, 58–59; normal man example, 55–56; pathological thirty-two-year-old lady example, 59–62; psychogalvanic experiment and, 62–64; stimulus words, 57–62; treating dream as, 94–99; tuberculosis, 64, 64n133; well-known psychologist example, 58
attitude, problem of, *xlviii*
Augustine, 50
Australian natives, murder and rage, 37–38
automatisme ambulatoire, 14

Bailey, Ruth, 5n34
Bally, Gustav, *xxix*
Barmen Declaration, *xxxi*
Barth, Karl, *xxxi*
Bavaud, Maurice, *xliii*
Baynes, Helton Godwin ("Peter"), *li*, 5n34
Beckwith, George, 5n34
Benares Hindu University, *xl*
Bergson, Henri, 19n59; intuitive philosophy, 19
betrachten: dreamer and, 101; as magical action, 98–99; word, 98
Black, Stephen, 48n112
blank slate (tabula rasa), 39
Bleuler, Eugen, *xlviii*, 14n50, 32n79
Boas, Franz, 4, 4n29
Boner, Alice, *xl*
Börsen-Zeitung (newspaper), *xxvii*
Bourget, Paul, 21
brain: thinking with, 15n54, 15–16; unconscious, 48
Brunswick, Ruth Mack, 25n70
Bugishu Psychological Expedition, 5n34

Capuchin monk, 87, 87n167
catatonic depression, 59
Catholic Church, 46; confession, 84–85
C. G. Jung Institute, *xlviii*
Character and the Unconscious (van der Hoop), 25, 25n70
Chennakesava Temple, *xli*
children, tabula rasa (blank slate), 39. *See also* family psychology
Children's Dreams (Jung), 50–51n118
chronology (1933–1941), *xxv–xlvi*
clairvoyants, second sight, 20
clan, collective unconscious, 53
Clark University, *li*, 4n29, 40n92, 74n149
Cobb, G. Stanley, *xxxvii*
Cohen, B., *xxix*
collective unconscious, *xxxviii*, *xlviii*, 49, *91*; analysis of, 54; archetypes, *li*; clan, 53; countries, 53–54; differentiation, 53–55; method of association, 55–56; motifs in, 100; problem of penetrating, 54–55; receptaculum of past, 49; shadow of future, 49–50; spiritus familiaris, 53
colonials: English children born in colonies, 3; psychology of, 4, 4n30
color: association experiment, 59; association with consciousness, *91*; psychology, 7; qualities, 32
Columbia University, 4
complexes: association experiment for discovery, 70; association experiment of conscious and unconscious, 79–81; dreams as, *lix*, 85–90; emotion, 80; existence of, *lviii*; "I" as, 82; individual, 83–84; memory, 80; primitives and devil possession, 81–82; Protestant church, 85; stimulus words, 83–84
Condillac, Étienne Bonnot de, 16n55; consciousness and unconsciousness, 16
Confessing Church, *xxxi*
consciousness, *91*; arrangement of functions, 20; collective unconscious, 49; complexes, 79–81; conception of soul, 13; dreams and mental illness, 14–15; emotions, 38, 39–40; feeling, 18, 26; functions of, 17–24, 27; "I" and individuality, 41–42; intersection of functions, 22–24; intuition, 18–19, 27, 35; invasions, 38, 40; Jung on, *lv*; memories, 38–39; personal and collective contents, 43; personal unconscious, 49; psychic functions of, 38; psychic thinking beyond, 15; sensation, 17, 18, 27, 39; sensation and intuition, 22; subjective part of, 38–39, 42, *91*; theory of functions, 36; thinking, 17–18, 26, 34; thinking and feeling, 20–22; thinking with brain vs. stomach, 15n54, 15–16; unconscious and, *lvi–lvii*, 12–13; unconscious state, 11
contagious effect, collective affair, 47–48
countries, collective unconscious, 53–54
Critique of Pure Reason (Kant), 36

Daily Mail (newspaper), *lix*
Daily Sketch (newspaper), *xxxvii*
Dana, Charles R., 26n71
Dasgupta, Surendranath, *xliv*
Descartes, René, 24n66
Deutsches Institut für psychologische Forshung und Psychotherapie, foundation of, *xxxvi*
Die Entdeckung der Seele (*The discovery of the soul*) (Adler), *liii*n21, 25
Dirac, Paul A. M., *xxviii*
Dollfuß, Engelbert, *xxv*; murder of, *xxxi*
dream psychology, association experiment, 85–90
dreams: affect dreams, 90; anxiety, 94; association of, 87; body stimulus dreams, 88–89; compass, *lx*; as complexes, *lix*, 87–88; consciousness and mental illness, 14–15; deciphering, *lx*; divining rod as magic wand, 97–98; flying, 44–45; ingestion, 89; interpreting, 99–101; knowing

dreamer, 92–93, 100; motifs in, 96, 97, 99, 100; mythology in, 96, 96n184; small and big, 86–87; somatic stimulus dreams, 88–89; stimulus words of, 88, 94, 95; treating as association test, 94–99; types of, 92; wish fulfillments and compensations, 89–90; writing down, 95
Dream Seminar, *xxxix*
durée créatrice, notion of, 19
Dwight Harrington Terry Foundation, *xxxix*

Edward VIII (King), *xxxviii*
ego, 82: "I", 38; will, 91
élan vital, notion of, 19
emotions: consciousness, 38, 39–40; stimulus words and emotional reactions, 63–64
Enabling Act (Ermächtigungsgesetz), *xxvi*
enantiodromia: Heraclitus, 8, 8n41; term, 8
energetics: law of energy conservation, 19–20n62; philosophy of, 19–20
extraverted/extraversion, *lvi*, 65

family psychology: association experiment, 75–78; father and children, 77–78; father complex, 77; husband and wife, 76; investigation of, 74–78; mother and children, 76, 78; reaction qualities, 74–75; studying, 71
family unconscious, 53
Federal Forestry Administration, 70
feeling: color of, 32; feeling-sensation type, 34; function of consciousness, 18, 26; intuition and, 32–33; psychogalvanic experiment for detecting, 62–64; unconscious, 31
Ferenczi, Sándor, *xxvii*
Fierz, Hans Eduard, *xxvi*
Flournoy, Théodore, *xlviii*
Flugel, John C., psychoanalysis, *li*
flying dreams, 44–45
Forel, Auguste, 14n50; case of automatisme ambulatoire, 14

Franco-Russian Alliance, *xxxiii*
free association, Freud's method of, *lix*
Freud, Sigmund, *xlii, xliv, xlviii*; Jung and, *xlix*, 8n39; method of free association, *lix*; Professor extraordinarius at University of Vienna, *l*
Fröbe-Kapteyn, Olga, *xlvii*
Frobenius, Leo, 50, 50n116; myth of sun hero, 50, 50n116
Fürst, Emma, 74n149

galvanometer, 62, 62n131
Geist, 8
General Medical Society for Psychotherapy (GMSP), *xxvi, xxvii*; German chapter of, *xxviii*
Georgia (ship), *xxxvi*
Gestapo, formation, *xxvii*
Gilli, Gertrud, *xliii*
Goethe: *Poetry and Truth*, 42n94; Stieler's portrait of, 22, 22n65; visions, 42
Gomchen, Rimpotche Lingdam, *xli*
Göring, Hermann, *xxviii, xlv*
Göring, Matthias H., *xxviii, xxxii, xlv*
Greek/Roman mythology, 96, 96n184
Grimm, Jacob and Wilhelm, 8n42
Guggenheim, Max, *xlix*

hallucinations, *xxviii*, 42
Hannah, Barbara, *li*
Harding, Esther, *xxix*
Harvard Tercenterary Conference on Arts and Sciences, *xxxvii*
Hauer, Jakob, *li*
Heimsoth, Karl-Günther, *xxxi*
Heraclitus, enantiodromia, 8, 8n41
Heyer, Gustav Richard, *xxix, xxxviii*
Hinkle, Beatrice Moses, 26n71
Hitler, Adolf, *xxviii, xxxi, xxxviii*
Holy Spirit, 46–47
Husserl, Edmund, *xlii*
hypnosis: confessions in, 70; somnambulistic persons, 13–15
hysterics, 81

"I": center of everything, 38; complex, 82; individuality and, 41; inner field of, 39. *See also* consciousness
IGMSP. *See* International General Medical Society for Psychotherapy (IGMSP)
Illustrated London News, 66n138
Illustrirte Zeitung (magazine), 66n138
immigrants: Americans, 3–4; going black under the skin, 4, 4n31
Indian Science Congress Association, *xxxix*, *xli*
Institute of Archaeology, *xxxix*
Institute of Medical Psychology, *xxxiv*, *xxxvii*
Internationaler Psychoanalytischer Verlag, *xxxv*, *l*
International General Medical Society for Psychotherapy (IGMSP), *xxxi*; Dutch national group of, *xxxiv*; Eighth Congress of, *xxxiii*; foundation of, *xxx*; foundation of Swiss chapter, *xxxii*; German chapter by Nazis, *l*; Jung resignation, *xliv*, *xlv*; Kretschmer and, 65n134
International Psycho-Analytical Association (IPA), *xxxvi*, *xlix*
In the Shadow of the Bush (Talbot), 51
Introductory Lectures on Psycho-Analysis (Freud), *l*
introverted/introversion, *lvi*, 65
intuition: Ahnung, 19, 20; clairvoyants, 20; color of, 32; concept of, 34; definition of, *lvi–lvii*, 35; function of consciousness, 18–19, 27; innermost of consciousness, 41; intuitive feeling, 32–33; knowledge, 35n84; sensation and, 22; unconscious, 28–29, 31
The Intuitive Basis of Knowledge (Lossky), 19
invasions: consciousness, 38, 40; unconscious, 42

Jacobi, Jolande, *xlvi*
James, William, 40n92
Janet, Pierre, *xlviii*, 81n160; analyse psychologique, *li*
Jesus, 47
Jones, Ernest, *xxxvi*, *l*
Joyce, James, *xlvi*, 29, 29n76
Jüdische Rundschau (newspaper), *xxxi*
Jung, C. G.: career events in chronology (1933–1941), *xxv–xlvi*; compromise formations, *lix–lx*; controlled association, *lix*; describing conscious and unconscious states, *lv–lvii*; existence of complexes, *lviii–lix*; Freud and, *xlix*, 8n39; giving interviews, *li–lii*; presenting self as scientist, *lii*; on psyche, *lv*; on psychology, *liv–lv*; *The Reality of the Soul*, *xxx*; recounting experiences, *liii–liv*; on unconscious, *lvii–lviii*; van der Hoop analysis with, 25n70
Jung, Emma, *xxx*, *xlvii*
Jung for Beginners, *lvii*

Kant, Immanuel, 36; obscure representations, 15
Kerényi, Karl, *xlvi*
Keyserling, Hermann, *xxxii*
Kirsch, James, *xxxi*
Knickerbocker, H. R., *xliii*
knowledge, types of, 35n84
Koch, Robert, 64n133
Köngener Kreis, *xxxviii*
Kranefeldt, Wolfgang M., *xxx*, *xlvii*, 25n69
Kretschmer, Ernst, *xxvi*, 65n134; types, 65

Lamaism, *lvii*, 32
Lange, Carl, 40n92
language: agglutinations, 79; alliterations, 79; association experiment, 78–79; complexity of psychic matters, 7; describing psychology, 6–7; perception with, 10; primitives, 37; words of humanity, 44
Lao Tze, 6n36

"Law for the prevention of hereditarily diseased offspring," Germany, *xxvii*
law of the series, *lvi*
Law on the "Reich chamber of culture," degenerate art ban, *xxviii*
laws of coincidence, *lvi*
League of Nations, *xlii*
L'Étape (novel), 99, 99n155
libido, concept of, 65
L'Illustration (magazine), 66n138
Locarno Treaties, *xxxv*
Lossky, Nikolay Onufriyevich, 19, 19n58
Ludger, Hans, 49n114
Ludwig (King) of Bavaria, 10, 10n45
lunacy, 15

magic, 30, 30n77; circles, 32; divining rod as magic wand, 97–98; dreamer with magic wand, 100–101
mana, 47; term, 20
manano, dream, 20
mandala, *lvii*, 32, 32n80
Mayer, Robert, 19, 19–20n62
McCormick, Harold Fowler, Jr., *xxxix*
medical psychology, 2–3
Mehlich, Rose, *xxxv*
memory disturbance, shock and, 69–70
Metamorphoses (Ovid), 92, 92n177
mirror galvanometer, 62
Mithras, 47
Morgan, Christiana, *xxv*, *xxix*
Münchner Neueste Nachrichten (newspaper), *xxxiv*
Munich Pact, *xlii*
Murchison, Carl, li, 1n25
mysterium coniunctionis, *li*

Nachträglichkeit, Freud's concept of, *lv–lvi*n22
Naef, Max, 14n50
Näf, Hans, *lix*
Nanjing Massacre, *xl*
National Socialism, *xlviii*; spiritual resistance of, *xxxi*

National Socialists, *xxv*, *xxxii*
Nazi Germany, *xxv*, *xxxiv*, *xlii*
Negroes, 5n34; collective matters stirring, 47–48; crossing bamboo forest, 52; dreams, 89; soul to God, 46–47; studying psychology of, 4n30, 4–5; thinking with stomach, 15, 16; unconscious thinking and feeling, 31; will and, 37
Neue Schweizer Rundschau (newspaper), *xxxv*
Neue Zürcher Zeitung (newspaper), *xxix*
Neumann, Erich, *xxxi*
neurosis, 55, 58, 81, 84, 93
New York Analytical Psychology Club, *xxxvii*
New York Times (newspaper), *xxxvii*
Nietzsche, Friedrich: intuitive type, 32; psychology, *liv*; *Zarathustra*, *xxix*, *xliii*, *xlvii*
Ninth International Medical Congress for Psychotherapy, *xxxix*
NSDAP, *xxvii*
Nuremberg Laws, *xxxiii*

The Observer (newspaper), *xxxiv*, *xxxvii*
Osmania University, *xl*
Ovid's *Metamorphoses*, 92, 92n177
Oxford Movement, 85n164

Paracelsus, *xlvi*
participation mystique, 46; husband and wife, 72–73; non-differentiation, 71–73
Pauli, Wolfgang, *xxxvii*
Pawlow, Iwan, *xxxv*
Perry, James De Wolf, *xxxvii*
personality, 15, 31, 65n134,
personal unconscious, 49; complexes of, 54
Pfister, Oskar, 32n79
Plato: eidola, 50, 50n115; on vision, 98n190
pneuma, wind, 8–9
Poetry and Truth (Goethe), 42n94

primitives: art of observation, 98–99; Australian natives and rage, 37–38; dangers of crossing a ford, 51, 51n120; devil possession, 81–82; feeling for psychic things, 86; language, 37, 79; rites of, 45–46; witch doctor and, 81
Proclus Lycaeus, 19, 19n60
Prohibition, repeal of, *xxviii*
psyche: human, *lx*; Jung on, *lv*; psychology, 1–2; "simple" tests, 10
psychogalvanic experiment, detecting feelings, 62–64
Psychological Types (Jung), 21n63, 25, 92n180
psychological typology, *xlviii*
psychology: complexity of psychic matters, 7–8; dream, *lx*, 85–90; Jung on, *liv–lv*; language describing, 6–7; medical, 2–3; prejudices against, 5–6; as psyche or soul, 1–2; representation of material, 6
Psychology Club Zurich, *xliv*
Psychology of the Unconscious (Jung), 26n71
psychoneurosis, 60
psychotherapy, Forel as pioneer of, 14n50
Pueblo Indians, thinking with stomach, 15–16

Radio Berlin, *xxvii*
reality, sensation, 2
The Reality of the Soul (Jung), *xxx*, *xlvii*
The Recreating of the Individual (Hinkle), 26
repression, 39, 48
reproduction experiment, 55
retrograde amnesia, 69
Riklin, Franz, 70–71n146
rising of sun, 46, 47
rites, primitives, 45–46
Rockefeller, John D., *xxxix*
Röhm, Ernst, *xxxi*
Röhm putsch, *xxxi*
roho (human breath), wind and spirit, 46
Roosevelt, Franklin D., *xxxviii*; New Deal, *xxvi*
Rosenthal, Hugo, *xxx*, *xlvii*
Royal Society of Medicine, *xliii*

saliva, 46–47
Sammlung Göschen (Kranefeldt), 25, 25n69
Schärf, Rivkah, 80n159
Schleich, Carl Ludwig, *xxxii*
Schmid-Guisan, Hans, 21n63
Schopenhauer, Arthur, 24, 32
Schrödinger, Erwin, *xxviii*
Schuschnigg, Kurt, *xxxi*
scientia intuitiva, 35n84
Secret of the Golden Flower (Wilhelm), *xliii*, *li*
Seelenprobleme der Gegenwart (Jung), 25
self-dissolution of Austrian parliament, *xxv*
Semon, Richard, 39n90
sensation, *lvi*, 91; color of, 32; function of consciousness, 16, 17, 18, 27; intuition and, 22; unconscious, 28, 28–29, 31
sensory perceptions, "I", 38
Seventh Congress for Psychotherapy, *xxx*
Shamdasani, Sonu, *xlix*
shell shock, 90
shock, memory disturbance, 69–70
shooting thaler, 70, 70n144
Société de Psychologie, Basle, *xxxii*
somnambulistic persons, hypnosis and, 13–15
Sonntagsblatt der Basler Nachrichten (journal), *xliv*
soul, 8; Aiolos as God of, 8–9; conception of, 13; etymology of, 8, 8n42; primitives and witch doctor, 81; psychology, 1–2; thinking and feeling, 21–22
Spinoza, Baruch de, 35n84
Spirit, wind, 8

spiritus familiaris, *lviii*, 53; habitual reaction of family, 72
Stieler, Joseph Karl, 22, 22n65
stimulus words: association experiments using, 57–62; breathing curve, 63; complexes evoked by, 83–84; of dreams, 94, 95; psychogalvanic experiment, 62–64; solving theft using, 67–70. *See also* association experiments
St. Jakob an der Birs, legendary battle of, 96, 96n185
Stockmayer, Wolfgang, 9n44
stomach, thinking with, 15n54, 15–16
Strauß, Walter, 34n81
Summer Olympics, Berlin, *xxxvi*
superstition, 29–30
Suzuki, Daisetz Teitaro, *xlv*
Swiss Academy of Medical Science, *xxviii*
Swiss Medical Corps, 48
Swiss Society for the History of Medicine, *xlvi*
synesthesias, 32

tabula rasa (blank slate), 39
Tao te Ching, 6n36
Tatbestandsdiagnostik: basis of, *lix*; diagnosis of evidence, *lviii*, 66
Tavistock Lectures, *lii*, 94n182
Tenth International Medical Congress for Psychotherapy, *xlii*
thefts, solving, stimulus words and reaction times, 67–70
thinking: color of, 32; function of consciousness, 17–18, 26; unconscious, 30–31; with brain *vs.* stomach, 15n54, 15–16
Thousand Mark Ban, *xxvii*
Tibetan Book of the Dead, *xxxv*
The Time Machine (Wells), 28
tuberculosis, 64, 64n133
Twenty-first Amendment, repeal of Prohibition, *xxviii*

ufgeisten, 8–9
ufgeistia, 8

Ulysses (Joyce), 29
unconscious: awareness during, 12–13; collective, 49, *91*; collective contents, 43, 44; compelling behavior, 46; complexes, 79–81; conception of soul, 13; consciousness and, *lvi–lvii*; creative activity of, 50; dreaming of, 11; feeling, 27, 31; functions of, 30–33; impressions from dream, 90; incursions, 42; intuition, 31; invasions, 42; participation mystique, 71–73; perceptions or impressions, 27–28; personal and collective, *lvii–lviii*, 49, *91*; personal contents, 43, 44; problem of penetrating, 54–55; psychic processes, 47; recognition of, 11; sensation, 28, 31; thinking, 30–31; thinking and feeling, 30
unconsciousness, intuition, 27
University of Calcutta, *xxxix*, *xli*
University of Leipzig, 97
University of Oxford, *xlii*
University of Travancore, *xli*
University of Vienna, *l*
University of Zurich, *xlviii*

van der Hoop, Johannes Hermanus, 25n70
Versailles Treaty, *xxxiii*, *xxxv*, *xxxviii*
Vishvanatha Śiva Temple, *xl*
vision, Plato's thought of, 98n190
Visions seminar, *xlvii*
von Franz, Marie-Louise, *xxix*, *li*
von Hindenburg, Paul, *xxv*, *xxxi*
von Koenig-Fachsenfeld, Olga, *xxxv*
von Ossietzky, Carl, *xxxiv*

Weizsäcker, Adolf, *xxvii*
Wells, H. G., 28, 28n73
Wildhaber, Ernst, 74n149
Wilhelm, Richard, *xliii*, *xlviii*
will, 36–37, *91*; human accomplishment, 38; reserve of, 37; volitional faculty, 36
wind, 8–9; spirit and, 46–47
Work Order Act, German, *xxix*

world events, chronology (1933–1941), *xxv–xlvi*
World War, 84

Yale University, *xxxix*

Zarathustra, Persian notions of, 19
Zarathustra (Nietzsche), *xxix, xliii, xlvii*

Zentralblatt (journal), *xxviii, xxx, xxxii, xxxv, xxxvi*
Zentralblatt für Psychotherapie (journal), *xxvi*
Zimmer, Heinrich, *xxvii, xlviii, li*
Zrvan akarana, idea of, 19, 19n61
Zürcher, Emil, 66n137; staging mock crime, 66–67

The Collected Works of C. G. Jung

Editors: Sir Herbert Read, Michael Fordham, and Gerhard Adler; executive editor, William McGuire. Translated by R.F.C. Hull, except where noted.

1. PSYCHIATRIC STUDIES (1957; 2d ed., 1970)
    On the Psychology and Pathology of So-Called Occult Phenomena (1902)
    On Hysterical Misreading (1904) Cryptomnesia (1905)
    On Manic Mood Disorder (1903)
    A Case of Hysterical Stupor in a Prisoner in Detention (1902)
    On Simulated Insanity (1903)
    A Medical Opinion on a Case of Simulated Insanity (1904)
    A Third and Final Opinion on Two Contradictory Psychiatric Diagnoses (1906)
    On the Psychological Diagnosis of Facts (1905)

2. EXPERIMENTAL RESEARCHES (1973)
    Translated by Leopold Stein in collaboration with Diana Riviere
    STUDIES IN WORD ASSOCIATION 1904–7, 1910)
    The Associations of Normal Subjects (by Jung and F. Riklin) An Analysis of the Associations of an Epileptic
    The Reaction-Time Ratio in the Association Experiment
    Experimental Observations on the Faculty of Memory
    Psychoanalysis and Association Experiments
    The Psychological Diagnosis of Evidence
    Association, Dream, and Hysterical Symptom
    The Psychopathological Significance of the Association Experiment
    Disturbances in Reproduction in the Association Experiment
    The Association Method
    The Family Constellation
    PSYCHOPHYSICAL RESEARCHES (1907–8)
    On the Psychophysical Relations of the Association Experiment
    Psychophysical Investigations with the Galvanometer and Pneumograph in Normal and Insane Individuals (by F. Peterson and Jung)
    Further Investigations on the Galvanic Phenomenon and Respiration in Normal and Insane Individuals (by C. Ricksher and Jung)

Appendix: Statistical Details of Enlistment (1906); New Aspects of Criminal Psychology (1908); The Psychological Methods of Investigation Used in the Psychiatric Clinic of the University of Zurich (1910); On the Doctrine Complexes ([1911] 1913); On the Psychological Diagnosis of Evidence (1937)

3. THE PSYCHOGENESIS OF MENTAL DISEASE (1960)
The Psychology of Dementia Praecox (1907)
The Content of the Psychoses (1908/1914)
On Psychological Understanding (1914)
A Criticism of Bleuler's Theory of Schizophrenic Negativism (1911)
On the Importance of the Unconscious in Psychology (1914)
On the Problem of Psychogenesis in Mental Disease (1919)
Mental Disease and the Psyche (1928)
On the Psychogenesis of Schizophrenia (1939)
Recent Thoughts on Schizophrenia (1957)
Schizophrenia (1958)

4. FREUD AND PSYCHOANALYSIS (1967)
Freud's Theory of Hysteria: A Reply to Aschaffenburg (1906)
The Freudian Theory of Hysteria (1908)
The Analysis of Dreams (1909)
A Contribution to the Psychology of Rumour (1910–11)
On the Significance of Number Dreams (1910–11)
Morton Prince, "The Mechanism and Interpretation of Dreams": A Critical Review (1911)
On the Criticism of Psychoanalysis (1910)
Concerning Psychoanalysis (1912)
The Theory of Psychoanalysis (1913)
General Aspects of Psychoanalysis (1913)
Psychoanalysis and Neurosis (1916)
Some Crucial Points in Psychoanalysis: A Correspondence between Dr. Jung and Dr. Loÿ (1914)
Prefaces to "Collected Papers on Analytical Psychology" (1916, 1917)
The Significance of the Father in the Destiny of the Individual (1909/1949)
Introduction to Kranefeldt's "Secret Ways of the Mind" (1930)
Freud and Jung: Contrasts (1929)

5. SYMBOLS OF TRANSFORMATION
   ([1911–12/1952] 1956; 2d ed., 1967)
   PART I
   Introduction
   Two Kinds of Thinking
   The Miller Fantasies: Anamnesis
   The Hymn of Creation
   The Song of the Moth
   PART II
   Introduction
   The Concept of Libido
   The Transformation of Libido
   The Origin of the Hero
   Symbols of the Mother and Rebirth
   The Battle for Deliverance from the Mother
   The Dual Mother
   The Sacrifice
   Epilogue
   Appendix: The Miller Fantasies

6. PSYCHOLOGICAL TYPES ([1921] 1971)
   A revision by R.F.C. Hull of the translation by H. G. Baynes
   Introduction
   The Problem of Types in the History of Classical and Medieval Thought
   Schiller's Idea on the Type Problem
   The Apollonian and the Dionysian
   The Type Problem in Human Character
   The Type Problem in Poetry
   The Type Problem in Psychopathology
   The Type Problem in Aesthetics
   The Type Problem in Modern Philosophy
   The Type Problem in Biography
   General Description of the Types
   Definitions
   Epilogue
   Four Papers on the Psychological Typology (1913, 1925, 1931, 1936)

7. TWO ESSAYS ON ANALYTICAL PSYCHOLOGY
   (1953; 2d ed., 1966)
   On the Psychology of the Unconscious (1917/1926/1943)
   The Relations between the Ego and the Unconscious (1928)
   Appendix: New Paths in Psychology (1912); The Structure of the
      Unconscious (1916) (new versions, with variants, 1966)

8. THE STRUCTURE AND DYNAMICS OF THE PSYCHE
   (1960; 2d ed., 1969)
   On Psychic Energy (1928)
   The Transcendent Function ([1916] 1957)
   A Review of the Complex Theory (1934)
   The Significance of Constitution and Heredity and Psychology (1929)
   Psychological Factors Determining Human Behavior (1937)
   Instinct and the Unconscious (1919)
   The Structure of the Psyche (1927/1931)
   On the Nature of the Psyche (1947/1954)
   General Aspects of Dream Psychology (1916/1948)
   On the Nature of Dreams (1945/1948)
   The Psychological Foundations of Belief in Spirits (1920/1948)
   Spirit and Life (1926)
   Basic Postulates of Analytical Psychology (1931)
   Analytical Psychology and *Weltanschauung* (1928/1931)
   The Real and the Surreal (1933)
   The Stages of Life (1930–31) The Soul and Death (1934)
   Synchronicity: An Acausal Connecting Principle (1952)
   Appendix: On Synchronicity (1951)

9. PART I. THE ARCHETYPES AND THE COLLECTIVE
   UNCONSCIOUS (1959; 2d ed., 1968)
   Archetypes of the Collective Unconscious (1934/1954)
   The Concept of the Collective Unconscious (1936)
   Concerning the Archetypes, with Special Reference to the Anima
      Concept (1936/1954)
   Psychological Aspects of the Mother Archetype (1938/1954)
   Concerning Rebirth (1940/1950)
   The Psychology of the Child Archetype (1940)
   The Psychological Aspects of the Kore (1941)
   The Phenomenology of the Spirit in Fairytales (1945/1948)

On the Psychology of the Trickster-Figure (1954)
   Conscious, Unconscious, and Individuation (1939)
   A Study in the Process of Individuation (1934/1950)
   Concerning Mandala Symbolism (1950)
   Appendix: Mandalas (1955)

9. PART II. AION ([1951] 1959; 2d ed., 1968)
      RESEARCHES INTO THE PHENOMENOLOGY OF THE SELF
   The Ego
   The Shadow
   The Syzygy: Anima and Animus
   The Self
   Christ, a Symbol of the Self
   The Signs of the Fishes
   The Prophecies of Nostradamus
   The Historical Significance of the Fish
   The Ambivalence of the Fish Symbol
   The Fish in Alchemy
   The Alchemical Interpretation of the Fish
   Background to the Psychology of Christian Alchemical Symbolism
   Gnostic Symbols of the Self
   The Structure and Dynamics of the Self Conclusion

10. CIVILIZATION IN TRANSITION (1964; 2d ed., 1970)
    The Role of the Unconscious (1918)
    Mind and Earth (1927/1931) Archaic Man (1931)
    The Spiritual Problem of Modern Man (1928/1931)
    The Love Problem of a Student (1928)
    Woman in Europe (1927)
    The Meaning of Psychology for Modern Man (1933/1934)
    The State of Psychotherapy Today (1934)
    Preface and Epilogue to "Essays on Contemporary Events" (1946)
    Wotan (1936)
    After the Catastrophe (1945)
    The Fight with the Shadow (1946)
    The Undiscovered Self (Present and Future) (1957)
    Flying Saucers: A Modern Myth (1958)
    A Psychological View of Conscience (1958)
    Good and Evil in Analytical Psychology (1959)

Introduction to Wolff's "Studies in Jungian Psychology" (1959)
The Swiss Line in the European Spectrum (1928)
Reviews of Keyserling's "America Set Free" (1930) and "La Révolution Mondiale" (1934)
The Complications of American Psychology (1930)
The Dreamlike World of India (1939)
What India Can Teach Us (1939)
Appendix: Documents (1933–38)

11. PSYCHOLOGY AND RELIGION: WEST AND EAST (1958; 2d ed., 1969)

WESTERN RELIGION

Psychology and Religion (the Terry Lectures) (1938/1940)
A Psychological Approach to Dogma of the Trinity (1942/1948)
Transformation Symbolism in the Mass (1942/1954)
Forewords to White's "God and the Unconscious" and Werblowsky's "Lucifer and Prometheus" (1952)
Brother Klaus (1933)
Psychotherapists or the Clergy (1932)
Psychoanalysis and the Cure of Souls (1928)
Answer to Job (1952)

EASTERN RELIGION

Psychological Commentaries on "The Tibetan Book of Great Liberation" (1939/1954) and "The Tibetan Book of the Dead" (1935/1953)
Yoga and the West (1936)
Foreword to Suzuki's "Introduction to Zen Buddhism" (1939)
The Psychology of Eastern Meditation (1943)
The Holy Men of India: Introduction to Zimmer's "Der Weg zum Selbst" (1944)
Foreword to the "I Ching" (1950)

12. PSYCHOLOGY AND ALCHEMY ([1944] 1953; 2d ed., 1968)

Prefatory Note to the English Edition ([1951?] added 1967)
Introduction to the Religious and Psychological Problems of Alchemy
Individual Dream Symbolism in Relation to Alchemy (1936)
Religious Ideas in Alchemy (1937)
Epilogue

13. ALCHEMICAL STUDIES (1968)

Commentary on "The Secret of the Golden Flower" (1929)
The Visions of Zosimos (1938/1954)
Paracelsus as a Spiritual Phenomenon (1942)
The Spirit Mercurius (1943/1948)
The Philosophical Tree (1945/1954)

14. MYSTERIUM CONIUNCTIONIS
([1955–56] 1963; 2d ed., 1970)
AN INQUIRY INTO THE SEPARATION AND SYNTHESIS OF PSYCHIC OPPOSITES IN ALCHEMY

The Components of the Coniunctio
The Paradoxa
The Personification of the Opposites
Rex and Regina
Adam and Eve
The Conjunction

15. THE SPIRIT IN MAN, ART, AND LITERATURE (1966)
Paracelsus (1929)
Paracelsus the Physician (1941)
Sigmund Freud in His Historical Setting (1932)
In Memory of Sigmund Freud (1939)
Richard Wilhelm: In Memoriam (1930)
On the Relation of Analytical Psychology to Poetry (1922)
Psychology and Literature (1930/1950)
"Ulysses": A Monologue (1932) Picasso (1932)

16. THE PRACTICE OF PSYCHOTHERAPY (1954; 2d ed., 1966)
GENERAL PROBLEMS OF PSYCHOTHERAPY
Principles of Practical Psychotherapy (1935)
What is Psychotherapy? (1935)
Some Aspects of Modern Psychotherapy (1930)
The Aims of Psychotherapy (1931)
Problems of Modern Psychotherapy (1929)
Psychotherapy and a Philosophy of Life (1943)
Medicine and Psychotherapy (1945)
Psychotherapy Today (1945)
Fundamental Questions of Psychotherapy (1951)

SPECIFIC PROBLEMS OF PSYCHOTHERAPY
The Therapeutic Value of Abreaction (1921/1928)
The Practical Use of Dream-Analysis (1934)
The Psychology of the Transference (1946)
Appendix: The Realities of Practical Psychotherapy ([1937] added 1966)

17. THE DEVELOPMENT OF PERSONALITY (1954)
Psychic Conflicts in a Child (1910/1946)
Introduction to Wickes's "Analyses der Kinderseele" (1927/1931)
Child Development and Education (1928)
Analytical Psychology and Education: Three Lectures (1926/1946)
The Gifted Child (1943)
The Significance of the Unconscious in Individual Education (1928)
The Development of Personality (1934)
Marriage as a Psychological Relationship (1925)

18. THE SYMBOLIC LIFE (1954)
Translated by R.F.C. Hull and others
Miscellaneous Writings

19. COMPLETE BIBLIOGRAPHY OF C. G. JUNG'S WRITINGS (1976; 2d ed., 1992)

20. GENERAL INDEX OF THE COLLECTED WORKS (1979)

THE ZOFINGIA LECTURES (1983)
Supplementary Volume A to the Collected Works.
Edited by William McGuire, translated by
Jan van Heurck, introduction by
Marie-Louise von Franz

PSYCHOLOGY OF THE UNCONSCIOUS ([1912] 1992)
A STUDY OF THE TRANSFORMATIONS AND SYMBOLISMS OF THE LIBIDO.
A CONTRIBUTION TO THE HISTORY OF THE EVOLUTION OF THOUGHT
Supplementary Volume B to the Collected Works.
Translated by Beatrice M. Hinkle,
introduction by William McGuire

Notes to C. G. Jung's Seminars

DREAM ANALYSIS ([1928–30] 1984)
Edited by William McGuire

NIETZSCHE'S *ZARATHUSTRA* ([1934–39] 1988)
Edited by James L. Jarrett (2 vols.)

ANALYTICAL PSYCHOLOGY ([1925] 1989)
Edited by William McGuire

THE PSYCHOLOGY OF KUNDALINI YOGA ([1932] 1996)
Edited by Sonu Shamdasani

INTERPRETATION OF VISIONS ([1930–34] 1997)
Edited by Claire Douglas

Philemon Series of the Philemon Foundation
General editor, Sonu Shamdasani

Children's Dreams. Edited by Lorenz Jung and Maria Meyer-Grass. Translated by Ernst Falzeder with the collaboration of Tony Woolfson

Introduction to Jungian Psychology: Notes of the Seminar on Analytical Psychology Given in 1925. Edited by William McGuire. Translated by R.F.C. Hull. With a new introduction and updates by Sonu Shamdasani

Jung contra Freud: The 1912 New York Lectures on the Theory of Psychoanalysis. With a new introduction by Sonu Shamdasani. Translated by R.F.C. Hull

The Question of Psychological Types: The Correspondence of C. G. Jung and Hans Schmid-Guisan, 1915–1916. Edited by John Beebe and Ernst Falzeder. Translated by Ernst Falzeder with the collaboration of Tony Woolfson

Dream Interpretation Ancient and Modern: Notes from the Seminar Given in 1936–1941. C. G. Jung. Edited by John Peck, Lorenz Jung, and Maria Meyer-Grass. Translated by Ernst Falzeder with the collaboration of Tony Woolfson

Analytical Psychology in Exile: The Correspondence of C. G. Jung and Erich Neumann. Edited and introduced by Martin Liebscher. Translated by Heather McCartney

On Psychological and Visionary Art: Notes from C. G. Jung's Lecture on Gérard de Nerval's "Aurélia." Edited by Craig E. Stephenson. Translated by R.F.C. Hull, Gottwalt Pankow, and Richard Sieburth

History of Modern Psychology. Lectures Delivered at the ETH Zurich. Volume 1, 1933–34. Edited by Ernst Falzeder. Translated by Mark Kyburz, John Peck, and Ernst Falzeder

Dream Symbols of the Individuation Process: Notes of the Seminars given by Jung in Bailey Island and New York, 1936–37. Edited by Suzanne Gieser

On Theology and Psychology: The Correspondence: The Correspondence of C.G. Jung and Adolf Keller. Edited by Marianne Jehle-Wildberger. Translated by Heather McCartney with John Peck

Psychology of Yoga and Meditation: Lectures Delivered at ETH Zurich. Volume 6: 1938–1940. Edited and introduced by Martin Liebscher. Translated by Heather McCartney and John Peck

GPSR Authorized Representative: Easy Access System Europe - Mustamäe tee 50, 10621 Tallinn, Estonia, gpsr.requests@easproject.com

www.ingramcontent.com/pod-product-compliance
Lightning Source LLC
Jackson TN
JSHW021902270525
84915JS00001B/2